NORTHWEST *of* SOMEPLACE

NORTHWEST
of
SOMEPLACE

Stories from roads less traveled

Volume I

by

Greg Frey · Chris Smith · Jon Osborn · Jake Smith

THE LOST BRANCH SPORTSMAN'S CLUB

All artwork by Chris Smith.

Some stories previously appeared in the following publications:

"The Swamp That No One Wanted" by Greg Frey	*Sporting Classics*
"Circling Back" by Jon Osborn	*Backcountry Journal*
"The Last Retrieve" by Chris Smith	*The Retriever Journal*
"The Light at Middle Ground" by Jon Osborn	*Sporting Classics*
"It's Not About the Buck" by Greg Frey	*Michigan-Out-of-Doors*
"Shifting Winds" by Chris Smith	*The Retriever Journal*
"Of Coffee and Creek Chubs" by Jon Osborn	*American Angler*

ISBN: 979-8-648-65468-6

Table of Contents

For our dads...

Jon Osborn I

Steve Smith

&

Norm Frey

Thank you for showing us this world.

Foreword

Police work is how I put food on the table (heaven knows it isn't hunting or fishing, or I'd be a whole lot thinner). Patrolling a beat can be demanding, but hats off to anyone who earns their daily bread with a pen. Like Hemingway said: "There's nothing to (it). You just sit down at a typewriter and bleed." Papa was right, of course, and lately I've needed the literary equivalent of a tourniquet.

Decades ago, I submitted an essay to Steve Smith, the godfather of outdoor writing and then-editor of *The Pointing Dog Journal* and *The Retriever Journal*. In response, he mailed back an encouraging letter saying, "You have talent, but you need direction. Come in and see me if you're ever up this way." In other words, "This ain't gonna cut it, kid, but keep at it."

Shortly thereafter, I drove up to Traverse City, and Steve gave me a tour of the publishing company and introduced me to his son, Jake, who held the position of managing editor. That afternoon, I walked out of the office with a signed copy of Steve's *The Whispering Wings of*

Autumn and a new sense of purpose. "I hope this elicits a career change," the inscription read, and in many ways, it did.

Fast forward nine years to the Kingsley Adams Festival. I was selling signed copies of my first book, *Classic Michigan Flies: 16 Legendary Patterns*, when I noticed a guy peddling some stunning paintings nearby. I'd seen enough of Steve Smith's books to recognize his kids anywhere. I knew this must be Chris, so I walked over and introduced myself. We hit it off like long lost brothers, and today I'm blessed to count him as one of my closest friends.

Around that same time, I began writing in earnest, and eventually queried *The Pointing Dog Journal* again. Either my skills had improved a bit or Steve and Jake took pity on me. One way or another, they ran the article. Over the years, I worked with plenty of editors and publishers. Some were great, others were tyrants, but few treated me as well as the Smiths. I never hesitated to send either of them questions, and they always responded quickly – a rare and welcome trait in this strange new world I'd entered.

Eventually, Chris and I began editing one another's writing, which has proven a Godsend. We often intertwine off-color humor amid the normal critique, and I can't count the times I've burst out laughing because of some lewd or preposterous "recommendation" that would make any editor seethe with rage – or worse.

Chris, an artist by trade, added writing to his repertoire with *Small Water Waterfowling*, along with a newspaper column and numerous essays and articles for various sporting publications. I still marvel at his ability to paint *and* write well. Truthfully, he has an overabundance of talent – like a successful actor who headlines Broadway musicals between movies. Sometimes, life just ain't fair.

Greg and I met by association through Chris and Jake – contacts which are highly suspect – but the fact that Greg fishes, hunts, and writes bodes well for his character, nevertheless.

So that's how I got mixed up with this group of raconteurs. Thanks, Jake, for drawing us together and dreaming up the idea for this book. Your edits made us appear at least semi-literate, and I'm honored to share a place amidst these pages alongside you.

—Jon Osborn
Holland, Michigan

. . . .

We live in two worlds at the same time – the physical reality, and the world of the mind. In my mind, I often travel to the wild places I love. That's a good thing because if it weren't for that, I wouldn't hunt, fish, and explore anywhere near as much as I do. These essays are a celebration of those places and the memories they've gifted.

I've been fortunate to collaborate with Jake, Chris, and Oz as we've shared a common love for all things wild and – in addition to faith and family – a common understanding of how important those things are to the core of our existence.

—Greg Frey
Petoskey, Michigan

. . . .

Whether paddling across a pond to reach a favorite duck blind, or weaving through a clearcut for a glimpse at a pointed grouse, I've always viewed time in the outdoors through an artist's eye. Simply put, I want to paint or draw everything. At the ripe-old age of six, my father encouraged me to draw the birds and dogs of *his* sporting adventures, which immediately became *my* sporting adventures.

Growing up with a dad who made his career as one of America's finest sporting writers, and a brother who was a chip off the ol' block, I found solace in the creativity of writing. With two such mentors, they gave me the boost to pursue putting pen to paper as a side job to my art.

The Lord certainly puts fine folks in our paths at the times when we need them. Fast forward some years later, when Greg's crooked smirk entered my life. I don't believe I've told him the influence he made, but I hope to someday. Further down the road, Ozzy showed up out of the blue, one of those *I just met you but have known you forever* moments everyone hopes to have at least once in their life. I'm still uncovering the blessing he's been. And then there's Jake, a brother *and* a best friend, who first thought of putting us together – four guys pushing 50 – to share our thoughts on the sporting world that has played such a large role in our lives, with hopes our ramblings resonate with others who feel the same.

I grew up reading the likes of Hill (even hunting with him a couple of times), Dad, McIntosh, Buckingham, and MacQuarrie. Fortunately, their words live forever in countless essays, articles, columns, and books, despite a steady decline in those who still turn their pages, or any pages, for that matter.

In a time when social media has made instant feedback, bragging rights, and a competition out of our beloved outdoor pursuits, I hope this appeals to anyone who goes to get away from it all, not bring it all with them.

We "brothers of the chase" put our waders on the same way, even though some leak more than others. Here's to the common ground we share, and the all-important perspective with which we view our experiences.

—*Chris Smith*
Suttons Bay, Michigan

. . . .

The first story I remember writing – like, *really* writing, trying to paint pictures with my words and connect the story to something deeper – was in the fourth grade. It was about a woodcock hunt where Dad shot a spindly aspen in half, bark exploding as if it had a firecracker lodged in it. I remember him later dropping a woodcock amid a shower of golden leaves and letting me pick it up. The story was a class assignment; I think I got a B+.

Writing became a part of me, as did reading some of the outdoor greats, of which I had one to tuck me in at night and take my brother and me fishing for bluegill and stuffing us full of cupcakes and Coca-Colas in glass bottles. Eventually, during my senior year of high school, I shared a few pieces with a managing editor friend working for Dad at then *Game & Gun* magazine. Greg Frey, a fellow bird hunter and trout bum, encouraged me, and he put in a good word for me at the local Orvis shop where he schlepped occasional hours for free flies. Greg, writing a column called "Diversions Afield" for a local small-town paper in our part of northern Michigan, also forwarded a couple of my stories to his newspaper editor, suggesting they needed a column from the next generation of writers. Thus, and quite originally, "The Next Generation" column appeared in the Lake Country Gazette. I'd never been prouder of making $15.

As lives are inclined to do, people spread out,take many roads, stay in touch, lose touch, connect on a holiday out of the blue. For me, that road included four years in Sault Ste. Marie for an undergraduate degree, two of those years spent with my brother, Chris. That simple decision turned out to be the best one I ever made when, in my first college class – Chemistry, no less – I saw a cute girl walk in the door. It took an entire year to be able to talk to her, and twenty-five years later, she's still one of my favorite hunting and fishing pals. We spent four more years together in South Dakota before moving back home and starting a family; and I made words a career at *The Pointing Dog Journal*, *The Retriever Journal*, and *Just Labs* magazine with Dad.

Chris and I have an incredible bond over everything, but especially hunting and fishing. His artwork continually amazes me, but his development as a writer is so reminiscent of our father. He's dragged me into remote places of the Upper Peninsula, Canada, and everywhere in-between – sometimes needing to twist my arm – and we've shared many hunting and fishing "firsts." When he struck up a friendship with Jon, it seemed like we'd discovered a long-lost brother. And when we reconnected with Greg after nearly twenty years, we *actually* discovered a long-lost brother. The e-mail and text banter among the four of us throughout this project has been nothing short of hysterical, at times appalling, and frighteningly identical in terms of quirks, jokes, pop culture references, what thrills our souls, and what drives us bonkers. Greg's joked that he feels like he's in a tree fort club.

It'll be fun to kick back this spring and catch some panfish together. Jon will supply the lake and boat, Chris the camera, and Greg the sarcasm.

I'll bring the cupcakes.

—Jake Smith
Traverse City, Michigan

Introduction

My dad – editor and founder of numerous sporting magazines, and author of thousands of articles and twenty-something books on our shared passions of hunting and dogs – told me he received his greatest compliment the other day regarding his writing.

It's when my 15-year-old son, Mark, giggled like a fool while reading Dad's 1986 book *Picking Your Shots*.

Many times, Mark came into the kitchen to read my wife and me a line or passage, ones I remember, vividly, reading the day the brand-spanking new books showed up on the doorstep when I was 12 years old. Mark found me in some of those stories. He laughed at Dad talking about hiding guns from Mom. He read about dogs I grew up with, coverts where I shot my first woodcock, and imagined his much-younger grandpa setting off into the woods looking not so much for birds but for a memory and a laugh. Exactly the way my kids and I do now.

I find the modern mountain of outdoor literature and media a conundrum, and at times I am perplexed as to why. And I say that as a provider of some of that literature. With so much more media available, it seems the world is absolutely exploding with information and stories about every possible aspect of hunting or fishing or shooting. Words and photos and videos are everywhere – to an almost absurd degree – with so much more detail and instruction and accessibility than at any other point in outdoor history. But in much of it, there still feels something *missing*.

Dad, Gene Hill, Corey Ford, George Bird Evans, Gordon MacQuarrie… they wrote for the everyman. Their hunts weren't outlandishly lavish, didn't explore new continents, weren't encounters with dangerous game, everything wasn't a trip of a lifetime or a bucket-list accomplishment. We joined them in their home places. Somehow, the way they conveyed their experiences – through the written word – made it clear that they chased the same game we did, saw the same scenes, felt the same ways.

Their stories fueled our passion without making us feel unworthy of carving out our own time in the outdoors if we didn't shoot a limit, bag a trophy, hunt somewhere exotic, have a perfect dog on point, and oh yeah, you'd better "post first and post most" to get more likes than the other guy and even better if you took slow motion video of the whole thing. It took a ridiculous amount of talent, but their words made us feel like we, too, could slip on a pair of worn leather boots, take a favorite gun we may or may not shoot very well, follow a happy dog having the time of her life through the woods, and miss a couple of woodcock. *And that that type of day was worth remembering.*

The world was smaller, more intimate, the experiences of the grouse covert or the duck blind or the trout stream reserved for our memories and our words and a handful of photographs in a journal.

We left the outside world out of our coverts and blinds and streams. Indeed, that was the very reason for going to those places to begin with.

Those places still exist. You can still go there to walk beneath a golden canopy of aspen leaves, or watch a front roll in and wait for ducks, or sit quietly – *quietly* – on the tailgate of the truck while petting the dog. And not everyone needs to know about it while it's happening.

That's how the idea for this little collection came about, from what we couldn't find out there that took us back to our youth, where we learned about the outdoors through the everyhunts of storytellers and by scratching out our own experiences. But mostly, the four of us simply had stories to share with one another – to catch up old friends and to make new ones – and we wanted to do it in its purest form, in a throwback to the written word and incredible artwork. And in doing so, we found that we'd all sort of chosen the same, rugged branch to follow on our life's hunting and fishing trail, the one shooting off from the main road of today's grandiose, splashy, instant gratification and toward the quiet and the small and the close. Indeed, this branch in the trail seems lost at times, as if there's only one road to take if you're to call yourself a worthy outdoorsman. But we found that branch in the trail. And you can, too.

So this is a book about dirty boots, muddy paws, and leaky waders, all taking us somewhere, leading us someplace… to that bird covert or trout stream we keep secret, to the duck or deer blind we cherish, and to the place where old dogs go to wait for us.

—*Jake Smith*

The Swamp That No One Wanted

I have made this pilgrimage to a cedar swamp off the shores of Lake Huron for twelve years. But this year is a milestone. The morning is quiet and clear, and with Gordon's rifle in my hand, I feel connected. Connected to Gordon, and connected to this swamp.

I work my way to the blind slowly, measuring each step and drawing in the still night air like a connoisseur swirling wine over his tongue. In the predawn grayness that infects the swamp, I feel a sense of well-being bordering on giddiness. This is opening day, and I'm in the midst of an event. After a half-hour of quiet plodding, I settle into the clump of balsams I call my blind and begin the waiting game.

These quiet hours in a cedar swamp give me time to rest and think. I'm one of those individuals best described as a type A personality – a spinning top whose life knows only two speeds. Maybe that's why hunting is so precious to me. Away from work and away from a home that needs work, I am doing something with a goal in mind; but the beauty of stand-hunting is that it requires sitting in complete silence without movement for hours at a time. Yoga without the spandex.

Almost imperceptibly, light begins to enter the swamp, as if someone is turning up a dimmer switch with the patience of the Creator. Only the sound of a red squirrel picking buds from the cedar behind me breaks the stillness of my swamp. I know there will be bigger bucks taken in Washtenaw, Van Buren, and Barry counties; but I will not shoot them. For me, deer hunting is not about big bucks. It's about home, and that is why I am here. So I wait, I think, and I remember.

A lot can happen in twelve years, and a lot has happened. For one, I lost my home. The folks retired, sold the ranch house, and left downtrodden Alpena for the coveted shores of Grand Traverse Bay. I still have a house, but not the one I was born in. Not the one in which I built the memories of childhood. My house is new to me. A stranger who, after five months, I'm beginning to trust, beginning to relax in. However, my second home remains. No one can sell my share in the Buck Hustler's Lodge.

This small cabin has been my hunting home for as long as I can remember. The building itself is not much to speak of – a dilapidated hodgepodge of clashing carpets, furniture that didn't sell at garage sales, and a tin Stroh's sign near the front door welcoming you to "The Friendliest Place in Town." But the cabin is not what draws me. It's the land.

If this humble mix of swamp and hardwoods in Sanborn Township is my home, then the cedar swamp on the back forty is my bedroom. Like the deer that inhabit it, to me the cedars mean refuge and cover, a place to shake whatever pursues me. Fortunately for me, not everyone shared my love affair with the swamp.

The original swamp consisted of nine members, and when I turned fourteen, I was assigned an abandoned wooden blind on the northeast corner of the property. Although it had produced nothing more than a button buck for its previous owner, I liked it. It was out of everyone else's way, and I was only a couple hundred yards from my father. While northern Michigan is known for outrageous deer blinds boasting everything from carpeting and insulation to televisions and Lazy Boy recliners, mine was not much to look at. Constructed of weathered gray barnwood, the four-foot-square box sat slightly tilted, and it wouldn't have taken a lot of huffing or puffing to blow it down. A piece of plywood kept my feet out of the mud, and a hard wooden bench kept me from falling asleep in the blind. At least the tar paper roof didn't leak.

I moved into the blind, and like a young woman sprucing up a dank cottage, I hung two posters of golden hardwood forests to brighten its dark interior. That first November, just days after being cut from the high school basketball team, the swamp delivered a spikehorn to me. It appeared between paragraphs of Ruark's *The Old Man and the Boy*, and with shaking hands I shot my first buck. As the recoil from the rifle drove me against the back wall, the gases blowing out the barrel ripped the posters from their thumbtacks beneath the window slits. I never replaced them, and two years later I left the confines of the blind to nestle myself between the trunks of three twisted cedars a few yards away. For seven years, the swamp delivered its yearly gift as a buck appeared on the overgrown logging trail.

Then one November they stopped coming. Life changed, and I entered a slump. The next four years became a blur. Depression, psychologists, graduation, advertising sales, instability with my relationships, my job, my future. It was sometime during those years that we decided to clear-cut a section of the property. The old cedars and aspen in the swamp had begun to tip over, leaving great craters that filled with tea-colored water in which nothing grew. The forester said it was time for new life. The aspens would grow, the deer would benefit. With death comes life. I consented, and over the course of a winter, a giant diesel skidder turned my portion of the swamp into a slash pile. The once-soft path meandering through a tunnel in the overgrown trees became a mess of jagged ruts and twisted brush. The funny thing was how small it all suddenly seemed. My quarter-mile walk from the end of the two-track to the blind turned out to be about a hundred yards.

I abandoned the clearing that now more closely resembled a war-torn French woodlot than the quiet cedar swamp I had once known. Hunting various sections of the camp, I hoped to find the hidden spot in which beauty and bounty joined. I wanted to hunt whitetails in the blazing hardwoods or near the trickling brook. I knew that deer liked these places, too, because I followed their tracks through them. The problem was they didn't like them in November. In November, they liked a swamp that was dark and safe.

It was shortly after the cedars were cut that Gordon Buxton gave us a gift. He was my father's boyhood mentor and a third grandfather to me. He lived across the road from my grandfather in southern Michigan. Whenever we went to see Grandpa on the farm, Dad and I always took time for a special visit with Gordon. He never had any children of his own and consequently gave all his love to us. His lungs had been filled with what can be lethal gas from fermenting silage in two separate accidents when he was young, and he had been a lifelong smoker. So we weren't surprised when the doctors said he had emphysema.

Gordon didn't make a big deal of the rifle. There was no solemn lecture or presentation ceremony. Just one day while Dad and I were helping him stack wood, he pulled a rotting leather and canvas case from his closet. Saying nothing more than he knew we would appreciate it and asking us to take good care of it, he handed us the rifle.

It wasn't a fancy gun. Simply a bluing-gone-silver .30-30 Winchester with smooth checkering from years of carrying it through the pines of Morley. I cherished that gun and only removed it from the cabinet to rub an occasional layer of oil on its cracked stock.

Spring came, and I decided to go back to college. Things began to look up. For the first time since early high school, I saw myself clearly. No longer the much-envied outdoor writer who would travel to exotic places and make a living on vacation, I envisioned teaching elementary children, and that seemed worth waking up for. I also found a friend who held my hand as we walked through the slash piles of my swamp and sat on the stump of the cedar that rested my back for seven years (I had forgotten to ask the loggers to save it). Together, we inspected the aspens that arose from their protective slash piles. There was light in the clearing that had once been my swamp, but I wondered if the clearcut would produce bucks as the swamp once had. Even if it did, I wondered if I would ever feel the comfort and security I did in the swamp.

When Gordon died, the rifle gained importance. Besides his fly rod and a pair of old leather bird-hunting boots, it was all I had left of him. With my throat choked as I stared down at him at the funeral home, I made a silent promise to shoot a buck with the rifle. One last deer for Gordon. I don't know why, but somehow it seemed important.

I hunted for an entire season with the rifle, carrying what I had created in my mind as the bridge between his world and mine. Many dark afternoons, I sat and watched snow collect on the rifle, melting into the cracked stock, making the wood appear almost black. As dusk came, I peered through the iron peep-sight, having difficulty distinguishing the front bead from the dark cedars, thinking of my new scoped .25-06 back home, wondering if this was such a good idea. But I had promised, and so I only hoped to see a buck before the stock split. It didn't, but as the season wore on and the slash piles became buried in bitter drifts that signaled the onslaught of an unusually harsh winter, no bucks appeared for me or for Gordon.

Some people measure their well-being in terms of money, but I'm not one of them. I measure quality of life in terms of stability in my relationship with my wife and career that allows me to leave both on November 15 and join Dad at deer camp. So as I sit nestled in a clump of balsams, I feel blessed.

In only four years, the aspens have sprung throughout the clearcut, all of them taller than me. I have finally given up wandering about the camp and returned to the clearcut in the middle of the swamp. Some careful investigation proved the deer had never really left, only changed their travel patterns.

Sunlight finally hits the tips of the cedars west of me. That sunlight has become the calling card of northeastern Michigan. In a marketing attempt to attract tourists who flock to the sandy shores and hardwood hillsides of western Michigan, the Chamber of Commerce has begun calling the state's eastern shoreline along Lake Huron "The Sunrise Side." Though the more affluent westerners make fun of Alpena's backwoods culture, it is the very undesirability of lowland areas like the one I sit in that has protected it from the commerce and developers who are building strip malls and subdivisions on those once beautiful hillsides of the Bay Region. So it is with my clearcut. No one wants to be here but me, and I am thankful for that.

The sun disappears beneath low clouds that spread across the November sky. Their ominous presence seems to warn of the coming hardship, and for deer and the many other animals that live here, the scarred clearcut and surrounding swap represent a stronghold of winter food and cover. Even northern storms cannot touch them here.

A snap catches my attention and pulls me from my thoughts. Everything else disappears, and my eyes and ears strain to locate the maker of the sound. Something rubs against branches. Then another snap. A deer is moving through the thick brush behind me, but before it enters the clearing, it stops. I raise Gordon's rifle and try to control the quick breathing that seems incredibly loud. There is movement, and the top of a young aspen begins to sway. I follow it to its base and see the head of a buck working against it. Still, I cannot risk a shot through the brush for fear of wounding the deer, so I wait in my tense crouch. After a ten-minute eternity, the buck steps back into the thick trees and heads north.

I do not know where or even if he will reappear, for he could follow any one of many trails that would take him along the edge of the clearing or back into the dense cedars. I do not hunt with bait and have nothing to lure him from the swamp other than chance.

But he does appear one last time, cutting across an inlet on the far side of the clearing, and in an instant the rifle is up, steadied, and fired. There is a quick crashing. Then silence. This time the careful walk across the clearcut is more difficult. My legs are shaking, and when I come upon the deer where it died at the base of a cedar, I sit down next to it and rest.

Its hollow hairs feel warm and soft. For a moment, I stroke it in respect and thanksgiving. Soon the work will begin. Cleaning and dragging the venison reminds me of Aldo Leopold's saying of how cutting your own wood warms you twice. So it is with the killing of a deer.

But for a brief while, I want to savor the moment. I am home, and I have just shot one last buck for Gordon. I wonder if he knows. I think it would make him happy. Whether or not it does, I cannot say, but I like to think so.

—*Greg Frey*

Daddy-Daughter Date

I'm claustrophobic, worry about my kids, hate flying, and drowning strikes me as one of the worst ways to go. So, naturally, I booked a fly-in, father-daughter fishing trip on a float plane only slightly larger than a matchbox car. Ah, the things parents do.

Truthfully, while I'd rather be trout fishing, one of those Ontario walleye trips has always piqued my interest. You hear stories about serene wilderness, fresh air, and fish jumping in the boat enough times that you just have to sample it for yourself, especially when a great buddy routinely heaps on the stories of his family's adventures in that part of the world.

But in a day and age when nothing's cheap, one has to be savvy when slipping said trip past the Good Wife. Luckily, kids are a perfect excuse. "Honey, I *need* to do this with Audrey, before she grows up and won't listen to me anymore." My wife, bless her soul, recognized years ago the importance of the paternal sporting bond and humors me when I come begging. All joking aside, if you're graced with kids who enjoy hunting and fishing, the outdoors quickly becomes one of *the* ways to strengthen your relationship.

Audrey was hooked on fishing, so to speak, at an early age by exercising the local bass and bluegill in the many lakes around our house. But at the impressionable age of thirteen, when dads commence their downward spiral into nothing more than an open wallet, time to deepen those parent-kid bonds is of the essence. With a young adrenaline junkie embarking on puberty, our normal excursions wouldn't suffice. Thankfully, I'd never experienced what we were about to – not even the float plane – so we had a rare moment to share something new together but, unfortunately, for which I could offer little comfort. Teetering on the scale of apprehension, I pulled the trigger.

The seven-hour drive from our northwestern Michigan home to the small lake airport in White River, Ontario, was a perfect distance. Few wilderness strolls are as pretty, with the gorgeous Laurentian Shield shoreline of Lake Superior eventually giving way to the impenetrable coniferous forests of south-central Ontario. We talked of how the native American tribes survived in such a place, with no roads, modern technology, or GPS to make life easier. She loved the extreme distances between towns. The different topography spurred questions. She was curious.

But all the while, an anxious anticipation hung inside the car like a third passenger, seat-belted in the back and quietly nagging. Upon reaching the small town, we located the "airport" a couple miles away, and that anxiousness quadrupled when our eyes simultaneously fell on the flying soup can of transportation we'd be boarding in less than twelve hours. And the even smaller watery runway. The owner/pilot came out of his home/office long enough to shake my hand, tell me when to be there, and then just as quickly departed.

A modest dinner in the town's only restaurant, and a couple beers for Dad, calmed some nerves; but lying in bed, they returned with a vengeance. My snoring daughter seemed ready, but the protective father was about to put us in the care of total strangers, with no reassuring stories to provide. The closest hospital was an hour away, and once we were at camp, that distance would increase by several hundred miles. What had I done?

Waking up to a windy morning finished off the night's fitful sleep. Little did I know, but float-plane pilots prefer a decent breeze to help skip off the water. With two planes moored to the dock, I relaxed somewhat when a pilot tossed our gear into the larger eight-seater. When another family drove up and commenced unloading as well, I breathed even deeper when overhearing it was an annual trip. After all, who would continue to trust an outfit that did barrel rolls with their guests and made you parachute from 5,000 feet to make camp? Surely, we were in good hands!

Cramming into a single-seated isle, Audrey strapped into the seat in front of me, our foreheads plastered to the window. Skipping off the waves, I knew the flight would be smooth when I had to ask if we

were airborne. With confidence, I must report it was the smoothest flight I'd ever been on, and we were treated to miles of green Ontario bush and pothole country, interrupted only by the
occasional moose. And in less time than either of us wanted, we were gliding into a small harbor that would be home for the next four days.

Reluctantly disembarking, we both admitted we could have spent the rest of the day doing touch-and-goes off the eleven miles of sprawling lake before us. But in no time, we'd squirreled away in our little cabin and unloaded the contents of a modest cooler of food brought from home to sustain us, with a devout goal to eat what we caught. I purposely did not include "dinner" food, knowing the ace up our sleeve was a fine chef at the main cabin who suggested we could always upgrade our "housekeeping" plan if we couldn't catch any fish. Challenge accepted.

Little did that chef know of my secret weapon: Audrey. The boat anchor had barely hit bottom when I heard the line that would be sweetly repeated every day: "Got one, Daddy!" I will be 80 years old and still remember how that made me feel. Watching her giggle as she pulled up that fourteen-inch walleye was worth every penny, and I quickly fell into the welcome pattern of putting minnows on her hook and netting her fish.

That sort of causal fishing from a safe boat under sunny skies – and no cell service, TVs, or computers – offered what I, as dad, was really angling for all along. We *talked*. Nothing earth-shattering, although I guess any conversation between a 46-year-old dad and his 13-year-old daughter could be thought of as just that, especially with so much competing for their attention.

After we caught enough for dinner each day, we explored. Small creeks held perch, beavers, and muskrats. We photographed and videoed dozens of loons, getting close enough that the possibility of one leaping into the boat was imminent. Auds discovered the joys of an open throttle on a good outboard and a light boat (something to remember when she gets her driver's license in a few years). We enjoyed a shore lunch on a hot day, finishing it off with a game of cribbage before continually jumping into refreshing water from a rock ledge fifteen feet up.

I watched my little girl become not so little, and more than once, wiped away some of her childhood through a sleeve of tears when she wasn't looking.

The morning of our scheduled departure brought about a somber mood – we were both homesick but could have stayed another week. This time, when the "smaller" four-seater taxied up to take just the two of us home, excitement replaced apprehension as we dove in, Audrey seizing the coveted co-pilot seat. She jabbered about the trip for hours on the way home.

That place was incredible. A conservative estimate of fish caught was in the hundreds, which says something for a fly-guy who's almost clueless with lures and bait. But it paled in comparison to the bond we strengthened. Driving home, she finally drifted off to sleep, and I let myself take that mental trip down the road a few years, when she'll be in college, and after, with a family of her own. I hope this adventure planted the seed for many more, with the *need* for Daddy giving way to simply wanting to spend time with me.

And she thought we were just fishin'.

—*Chris Smith*

Circling Back

"Some people ask why men go hunting. They must be the kind of people who seldom get far from highways. What do they know of the tryst a hunting man keeps with the wind and the trees and the sky? Hunting? The means are greater than the end..."

—Gordon MacQuarrie

Nothing in nature is static; the outdoors is in a perpetual state of flux. Likewise, the journey through hunting is an evolution. Everyone's path looks a little different, but somewhere along the way, *why* supersedes what, where, when, and how. For some, this watershed moment happens in a duck blind; for others it occurs at deer camp or behind a pointing dog. In my case, a squirrel kick-started my hunter's heart into motion.

Growing up in the '80s, a few neighborhood kids had swimming pools, some passed the hours playing Atari video games, and still others owned boom-boxes – all the better for blaring Air Supply or

John Cougar Mellencamp. But my best buddy had something even better – a field. Tim's family didn't actually *own* the rolling prairie behind his house, but everyone referred to it as "Tim's Field" anyway. Back then, folks seldom fretted over property lines.

By age eleven, we kids had explored every creek, pond, and woods within walking distance of home; but branching out only solidified our feeling that Tim's Field was the greatest place on earth. Even now, the memory remains fresh as ever. I close my eyes and smell the yeasty aroma of knapweed baking in the summer sun while bees drone among the poppies. That field was our own private wilderness, an uncharted no-man's-land where we slept beneath the stars, learned the finer points of campfire cookery, and resolved rare disagreements with foul language and fists. Above all, it's where we grew into hunters.

In that innocent, pre-Columbine era, almost every kid owned a BB gun, but Tim and I had grown tired of our anemic, spring-powered Red Ryders. The neighborhood hardware store offered other, more powerful options; but paperboys didn't earn much money, especially fat kids like me who squandered most of their income at the candy store. With a little fiscal dedication and sacrifice, I could afford a shiny new Benjamin – the apple of my eye – but my sweet tooth won out in the end, so I opted for a more affordable Daisy Power Line 880.

By the summer of '86, I'd finally saved enough cash – around $50, if memory serves correctly. Tim, who lived a frugal lifestyle, had socked away enough to buy the rifle, ammo, *and* a Simmons scope. So, cash in hand, we peddled our bikes to the hardware store to upgrade our armament.

Fast forward a few months to late autumn. The seasons were teetering between fall and winter. As the light faded from the slate-colored sky, Tim and I were patrolling his field with our pellet rifles. A line of Osage orange trees bordered the western edge, and their bare branches clicked together in the chilly breeze. Looking up, we spotted a busy fox squirrel silhouetted against the skyline. Until then, our shooting had been limited to faded Schlitz cans and a few unfortunate starlings; but we'd read every issue of *Field & Stream*, and the notion of procuring meat for the table was alluring.

From where we stood though, we were a long way off from squirrel stew. To the casual suburbanite, city squirrels seem downright tame, but truth is, the hardscrabble, rural variety are wary as whitetail bucks. Snap the tiniest twig or scuff a dry leaf and they beat feet in an awful hurry. With that in mind, we crept carefully through the weedy underbrush, closing the distance. But another issue loomed ahead. Even charged with ten pumps, those pneumatic rifles barely generated much power, and squirrels were tough. What's more, the single-shot 880 was only slightly quicker to reload than a Civil War musket.

What transpired next was neither quick nor humane. Supercharged with adrenaline, our misses exceeded our hits, and even the pellets that struck home weren't immediately lethal. The squirrel finally succumbed to the air rifle version of *Lingchi*, or, "death of a thousand cuts." Given the violence we'd inflicted, our journey into blood sport might have ended right then and there. But ours was a childhood steeped in Jim Bridger and Jeremiah Johnson, so we hiked back to the house, swinging our trophy by its rusty-brown tail.

Home were the hunters.

Arriving at Tim's garage, we found ourselves at a loss for how to proceed next and began rifling through a dog-eared Boy Scout manual. (This was back when the Scouts actually encouraged survival skills.)

Following the field-dressing instructions, we removed the innards and wrestled the hide off, agreeing that the process looked much easier in print. Next, we consulted Tim's mom, who, as a former farm girl, knew just what to do. She soaked the carcass in saltwater, browned it hot oil, and placed it in the oven. The end result was delicious, so memorable, in fact, the details remain vivid to this day. Somehow, we knew we'd heaped a lot on our plates, and food was only the half of it.

Ancient man never questioned why he hunted. Back then, killing and eating meant survival. But as time passed, cultures evolved, and farms and supermarkets displaced the need for wild protein. That anyone would dispute hunting's validity today speaks volumes about modern society's access to sustenance. Think about it: Food (or some synthetic version of it) is available at every corner store, gas station, and vending machine – endless, empty calories at arm's reach. Hunting, on the other hand, is arduous, uncomfortable, and messy. There's no guarantee of success, and it's so much easier to buy styrofoam-packed meat. No fuss, no muss, no blood on your hands; so why even bother?

Why? The answer is infinitely more complex than killing and eating, yet simple at the same time. Hunting has been seared upon our DNA since the dawn of time, and those lingering, primal instincts prove we were created to be active participants, not mere spectators. In fact, every aspect of hunting flies in the face of a modern society bent on instant gratification; rebellion rendered to its purest form. And that's why, in this empty era of skyscrapers, sidewalks, and cell phones, we are hunters still.

It's also why we circle back.

Jump ahead to 2019. It's February, and we're hunting squirrels in the river bottoms south of town. Tim's stuck at work, so it's just Kirk and me. We both own scoped .22s – perfect rifles for the job – but the recipe we're craving calls for a decent amount of meat.

Tomorrow's forecast and the glowering western sky affirms the weatherman's snowy prediction. You can smell it in the air and feel it in the breeze. Something's brewing. We know it, and the squirrels feel it, too. All morning long, we catch them in the corn stubble, filling their cheeks with last year's crop. They're reluctant to stray too far from the treeline, but if we stay low and walk the gullies, sometimes we get lucky.

Hunting these hillsides calls for one of two methods – sometimes sitting and waiting works best, but today's a day for stalking. Make no mistake, this style of hunting isn't for the faint-of-heart; once a farm-country fox squirrel knows you're there, the race is on. Then it's flat-out running and gunning. To ensure a successful shot, we have to close the distance within 50 yards, but 40 yards is preferable. It's always a moving target, more like wingshooting than anything else.

My grandpa always said, "There's a tool for every job," and nothing beats a choke-bored scattergun filled with heavy No. 5s. Shotguns are a lot like hunting buddies – there's no friend like an old friend – and nothing drives this point home better than the ancient Winchester I'm carrying. This trusty corn-sheller was purchased by a friend in Park Falls, Wisconsin, sometime during the Truman administration. My old pal carried it nearly 50 years but recently turned it over to me. Park Falls may be "The Ruffed Grouse Capital of the World," but this particular model was probably intended for ducks and geese, not fast-flying pa'tridge. Thing is, the dense patterns work perfect for squirrels.

When John Browning first introduced the Model 97, it quickly found favor with sportsmen and market hunters. Back then, you could order guns almost any way you liked, and this one rolled off the factory floor with a 30-inch, full-choked barrel, wearing a price tag of $27. No chump change in 1921, but Winchester would crank-out over a million of these iconic hammer guns during the 97's 60-year life-span. Fortunately, a half-century later, a few are still floating around the used market.

But back to the squirrel hunt. By the end of the day, we're drenched in sweat, but our game bags hang pleasantly full. The fruits of our labors are destined for the stewpot, where robust, wild flavors mingle with carrots, celery, and herbs. After simmering all day long, the concoction will be poured over biscuits and mashed potatoes. But a single dinner will hardly be the final product. The bones, along with last fall's grouse, woodcock, and ducks, will make a batch of homemade game stock, to enhance future feasts. Even the spikey fur and rusty-red tails won't go to waste – they'll be repurposed into streamers and nymphs to seduce bluegill, bass, and trout come springtime. That's about as "farm-to-table" as it gets.

I'm in my forties now, firmly entrenched in that strange acid-trip known as Middle Age. The Daisy Red Ryder, Power Line 880, and my hair are long gone. Tim's Field is a condominium complex now, but its influence lives on. It's where I was born a hunter – and the *why* hasn't changed a bit. Of course, you never really go home again, but sometimes you circle back and recall exactly what it was like to be there.

What I wouldn't give for that old Daisy pump and even five more minutes in Tim's Field.

—*Jon Osborn*

A Shot Not Taken

Dad came home early from work in time to find me sitting behind a pile of hunting gear and lacing up my boots. At my feet lay cased guns, orange vests, a shell bag, water for the dogs, Dad's knee-high rubber "Wellies," and his light blue hunting shirt.

Nosing under my chin, Chris's black Labrador, Maggie, scarcely let me see my boot laces, determined that I notice how badly she wanted to go. Dad's veteran English setter, Jess, sprawled atop the hunting vests, contented – she knew the only way to get the gear was through her. She perfected this trick over her nine seasons in the uplands.

"Very good, my boy," Dad remarked, climbing the few stairs to the living room and noticing the preparations. He set his soft-covered briefcase against the wall. Mags – three years old and still a puppy in so many ways – rushed to him, spun a few circles, and leaned heavily against his leg, grunting in thick pants in her excitement. Jess just lifted her head and thumped her tail on the shell bag. She still wouldn't move, not until the front door opened and the gear moved out of the house. "Let me make a sandwich, and we'll be off," Dad said, scratching Maggie's ears and reassuring her. She spun in tighter circles and widened her jowls into a Labrador smile.

"Already packed," I said, bringing out a brown paper lunch sack from behind the two-liter bottle filled with water. "There's a couple of Cokes in there, too. All you need to do is get changed." Dad didn't waste time with an approval; he gathered up his hunting clothes and disappeared into the bedroom while I loaded the trunk of his blue station wagon. The dogs busted out the door first.

Within minutes, Dad waved back at Mom, who hollered after him to be careful. She always points a crooked finger straight up at us with such instructions: "Be careful"; "Watch your gun barrels"; "Do you have water for the dogs?"; "Do you have your license?"; "If the weather looks bad, come back." We just bow our heads and smile; she feels better giving us an earful about safety before we leave, and we appreciate it, mockingly sometimes. And sometimes, our licenses *were* left on the bedroom dresser.

Jess and Mags lumbered into the hatchback and sat on top of the gear, but we put our gun cases in the backseat. Dad made certain nothing scratched the rectangular leather case with the worn brass buckles that housed his 16-gauge Webley and Scott side-by-side.

Made by some of the finest London gunmakers circa 1920 – and with a mysterious but no doubt steeped history – the light double found itself on Dad's radar back when timing and money rarely coincided. But they did this time, and the gun and oak-and-leather case made the trip from Scotland. It took much reconditioning to get it back to its almost original state, but the investment had been worth it.

Dad wielded this piece of art with stunning accuracy, and it most assuredly will find its way down through generations of many Smiths to come.

He saved it for sun-drenched days during the ruffed grouse and woodcock season, when the elements wouldn't test the London finish on the elegant English walnut stock or the near perfect blueing on the sleek, twenty-eight inch barrels. Occasions when the October sky held a few cotton-ball clouds and the leaves rippled in all their resplendent autumnness, a slight breeze producing a cascade of color. After inhaling the covert's aroma, Dad would unbuckle the weathered case, put on his shooting gloves, and tenderly remove the stock and barrels. Gently, he'd slide the barrels into the lock at the breech, snap them up, and click the thin splinter forend into place with a steady squeeze. Turning the smooth lever, he'd drop the barrels, cocking the firing pins with an audible *click*, and slide two blue or purple or black shells into the chambers, their brass glinting back the October sunshine.

Then, Dad would stare at the gun, wondering what stories that gun could tell, how many birds it had shot, if it had seen driven pheasants in Scotland's moors, or maybe it had been the possession of a gamekeeper of a castle on a large estate. Like other old guns, you look at them and imagine their lives: Perhaps that Parker or Fox made its way across the continent in fits of short employment with various hunters – a New England grouse gun when the hunting clothes were still breaks and tweed jackets; a Georgia quail gun in an era when the horses pulled the hunters in wagons while the dogs worked the coveys of bobwhites; maybe even a Kansas pheasant gun about the time the birds kept a man in the fields most of the day. For Dad, that Scott is his beautiful October day grouse and woodcock gun.

Which was exactly what we drove through. It was also October Third, a family tradition as steeped as the Scott's. October Third always found us in the grouse and woodcock coverts, regardless of the weather. It's why Dad cut work three hours short, and why I'd raced home after school without lingering in the hallways. October Third was an occasion to embrace the season, and we did it the best way we knew how – by walking through the bracken ferns and alder runs and aspen cuts, hoping for a thunder flush or twittering wings. Only one thing lacked that October Third – Chris. He was up at college, carrying on the tradition with a hunt of his own.

I'd handle Maggie, something I hadn't done too regularly. She'd follow commands from just about anybody, though, and she had enough of these excursions under her collar to know the game – she stayed close, sniffed for the good smells, and got to feel warm feathers when Dad's gun went off.

Dad would take Jess, as always. She was slowing down in her age, which made Dad remark that they made a perfect old pair together, both sauntering through the woods at their own pace instead of racing behind a retriever that had the gall to actually make the birds fly. Not Jess. Not his setter. She fit perfectly with the London gun – a couple of English prim and propers who did things the *right* way or didn't bother with them at all. Growing up behind her staunch points, I think I learned as much from her about doing it the right way – with respect and honor and courtesy.

The station wagon turned off the pavement onto a wide gravel road. The dogs immediately sat up, panting, wet noses smudging the back window and hot breath fogging the glass. In a few miles, we turned onto a rutty two-track, its entrance marked by a row of towering white pines. I'd discovered the covert on a scouting trip in

August, and it turned out to be pretty good – my first grouse and woodcock covert contribution to the family. We followed the trail – or what passed for one – about two hundred yards into the heart of a mosaic of aspen cuts, pulled off into the bracken ferns, and stopped.

We sat in flickering shadows as the breeze swayed the trees. The orange and yellow leaves brushing against each other sounded like an endless wave, and some broke from the branches and fell in spirals. The smell hit me when I opened the door, that familiar scent of dank earth and dry brush and other forest odors. It's the cool aroma of October, of hunting season. I wish someone could bottle it.

The dogs cared about only one thing, though – getting out of that hatchback. Maggie leapt out, but Jess oozed out of the back before scampering around the car, waiting for her bell. It *clanged* as Dad removed it from the shell bag, and she strode up to him and sat; ears down, she craned her neck, and Dad slipped her head through the collar. In a flash, the nine-year-old setter was off – no sign of her aging arthritic bones slowing her down, at least for the moment – and the bell greeted the woods with a tinkling that sparkled like the autumn colors.

"Stay close, Jess," Dad muttered. Jess had perfected the art of selective hearing in the house – listening only to what she felt benefited her sleeping arrangement or stomach in some way – but in the field, all business. She scampered back through the ferns and sat by the opened hatchback, waiting for the command to begin.

Maggie, on the other hand, rushed around in heavy grunts and pants, *snarfing* each bush, leaving her mark in at least a half-dozen spots, possessed. After a few hollers for her to calm down, she at last came by my leg to heel and waited. I noticed Jess glare up at Dad, who shook his head at her. *Retrievers*, they seemed to say to each other.

Our vests on, I put together my light 20-gauge double. Dad brought his case to the back, and in no rush, he uncased and assembled the Scott, pausing with it broken over his arm to recall its dubious history, and then, grinning, he gazed skyward into the trees. He took off his tweed hat festooned with hat pins – a small wooden grouse feather, a tiny brass shotshell, a copper plate from a quail plantation, and many others – and drank in the scent of October Third. "Now this is much better than the office," he said before gently closing the breech on the Scott.

We walked down the two-track for a bit before heading into a cut of young aspen. Mags scampered off in front of me, a black blur through the ferns. Jess *clang*ed her way ahead of Dad. The bell provided a razor's edge of anticipation – any second, it might go silent. For a moment, it did, but Jess was simply watering the leaves.

I needed to keep an eye on Maggie, though. She didn't provide much warning of an imminent flush save for her hollow *snuffs* and a hyperactive tail. For a while, I followed her by the zigzagging bracken ferns as she lumbered through them. It worked just as well as the bell.

Finishing out the first covert without a flush, we met on the trail and walked side by side again, sometimes giving faint whistles for the dogs to get back in there and "hunt 'em up." Dad rested the broken Scott over his shoulder; my 20-gauge dangled in my right hand by my waist. It was nice to finally see some leaves off the trees, which suffered under a blanket of frost for a few nights. The ferns still stood, but the thinning tree branches allowed at least a chance to glimpse a fleeing grouse or a towering woodcock compared to the green jungle of early season.

"You take Maggie on that side; Jess and I will go through this patch," Dad instructed with a wave of his hand. I whistled to Mags, and she followed me into the ferns and thinning aspens on the right side of the trail. Dad and Jess strode off into a thicker, mid-aged aspen stand ablaze in yellow on the opposite side.

I stumbled in a few holes, even fell right to the ground at one point. With a retriever, it's harder to watch where you're going since your eyes are glued to the dog. You could find each foot behind Jess – her bell told you everything. Mags ventured ahead a bit too far while I took it slow, so I reigned her in with a few soft toots on the whistle. That's when I saw the ferns, moving toward me as if in the wake of a shark, spin and go in the opposite direction. Birdy.

Out of the corner of my eye, I caught wings – a grouse fluttering along the fern tops fifteen yards away. Not nosed into the air by Mags, otherwise it would've flushed much more vigorously, it obviously had been disturbed by our approach. But I'd never seen a grouse fly that way: It fluttered about six feet off the ground, like a sparrow might flit from bush to bush. It seldom beat its wings, gaining the air it needed from a first few silent flaps and then gliding along the fern tops, even brushing a few. Maggie still *snarfed* where it sat, so it presented a

clear shot. It was flying so slowly, I raised the twenty and actually put the bead on his head.

I stopped. An unsporting shot; grouse murder. Ruffed grouse were supposed to thunder forth from their hiding spots, put the fattest tree between you and it, and vanish into denser parts of the forest. This bird – obviously not crippled – nonchalantly glided through an open lane in the thin aspens, as if unsure why it felt the need to flush in the first place. A straightaway open grouse shot, something you dream about but rarely experience. And still, I lowered my gun.

It headed toward Dad, or, more precisely, about forty yards ahead of him. The ferns swallowed up the bird. "Dad," I said as quietly as I dared. "Grouse in front of you. It just fluttered ahead; Jess should run into it any second." I whistled Maggie in toward me, letting Jess have her turn instead of cutting the Labrador loose on the scent.

I stopped and followed the entire episode with my ears: Jess's bell *clanged* regularly as she cantered through the woods. They slowed until finally, silence, the endless wave through the tree branches once again the only sound. "Point," Dad said in a flat tone. I knew he gripped the Scott a little tighter, calling into action the gun's pragmatic function. The gun was a thing of beauty, but it was also a gun, with a utilitarian purpose – meant to be admired, sure; but also used.

"Be ready in case it cuts back toward you," Dad said. I tucked the twenty under my arm, like waiting for a clay bird to be pulled. Mags sat at heel.

Dad moved forward, the dry brush crunching underfoot, and then, the intoxicating thunder flush. The pounding wings were brief, then silent – the bird made a commotion only while rising through the jungle of ferns, but it obviously flushed with more intensity than when it did in front of me. The Scott splintered the crisp October air.

"Dad?" I asked, my heart throbbing.

"Wing-tipped him," Dad said. "Get Mags up there." I heard him already running up to where he'd seen the bird go down.

I stumbled catching up. Maggie heard the shot and knew what it meant; she also read my recklessness through the woods and scampered ahead and caught up to Dad just as he found Jess.

The old setter scurried ahead with the flush, her bell ringing furiously; she didn't retrieve, but she did point dead birds for the most part, helpful with a crippled bird – like now. We found her solid, pointing into a thick entanglement of ferns.

"Steady," Dad whispered. "Jake, be ready. He might flush again." He slipped another shell into the empty right barrel.

But Mags knew her job. She loped up, took a look at Jess, and followed the setter's stare into the ferns. The black dog ran up to her, sniffed Jess once, and put her nose to the ground right where Jess pointed. Her tail spiraled in wicked circles – her nose full of grouse scent – and her whole body trembled. She disintegrated into the ferns, her nose on the ground.

I started to follow, but Dad pulled me back. "Just let her work." Having hunted behind more dogs than I could ever hope to, he knew the capabilities of a well-trained dog when she let her instincts take over. The only way she wouldn't come up the bird was if it had skulked ahead and reflushed unseen.

I watched the action of the ferns. They didn't zigzag as much but moved more in a straight line. Then a hard right turn, then back to the left. Then a diagonal off to the right. Out ahead thirty yards now, Jess still frozen, Maggie *snarfed* and *huffed* at each step. The ferns shot back left again, then straight away. *How fast do grouse run?* I thought, desperately wanting to hurry ahead and help the dog.

"She's on him," Dad said calmly. He broke the Scott over his arm. I still gripped mine in the ready position but relaxed when I saw the ferns cut once more to the left and stop. Forty yards ahead, the ferns parted in a circle and waved with Maggie's tail.

Slowly, the ferns moved back in a straight line toward me. I bent down underneath their canopy and shouted, "Come Mags!" I looked back at Jess, who sat and panted next to Dad's leg. She knew Mags held the bird now. A flash of black flickered in the ferns ahead, which then parted and the Labrador emerged, prancing toward me, her ears back and eyes wide and a still alive ruffed grouse in her mouth.

I took the bird from her; it died when I grasped it. "Good girl!" Dad reached over and ruffled her ears, chuckling. Mags panted and waged so hard her rear end wiggled almost out of control. I handed Dad the large gray-phased bird, and he gently stroked the feathers back into place, lowered it down to Jess, up on all fours and straining for a whiff. She buried her nose into the feathers and gave it one good *snuff* and a lick, then she *clanged* off into the ferns as Dad slipped the bird into his game pouch.

"It flutter-flushed in front of me back there, and I put the bead right on his head. But it wasn't a sporting shot, and I saw you two were going to get a chance at him. So I let him go," I explained. "It just wasn't a fair chance."

He smiled approvingly. "That's the whole name of the game," he said. "Sportsmanship. You showed a lot of maturity by not taking that shot."

Those words rang in my ears the rest of the hunt, of which we flushed two more grouse, heard but not seen. But we found their dust bowls, something I'd never discovered before. At the base of a rotting log sat two depressions, grouse feathers scattered about, where the birds bathed in the dust, cleaning up their feathers of various insects. We had interrupted, and they escaped with a chiding flush.

We found the trail leading back to the car, through the aspen cuts we hunted initially. Maggie spun through them again; Jess sauntered ahead, slipping back into her selective hearing and ignoring Dad's call to heel.

Sometimes, by not pulling the trigger, we open ourselves up to a whole new realm of experiences. Perhaps, if we don't drop the hammer on a cupped hen mallard, she'll sit and chatter with us in the decoys for a while. Maybe letting a twittering woodcock escape through an alder run will present a young hunter his first opportunity at a bird later on. Letting a cackling rooster flee across the corn stalks might be our way of giving a bit back in return for all his brethren we've taken throughout the season. It's a mark of voluntary restraint, a sign of a greater ethic we hold ourselves to that must be integral to the hunt.

By not taking that shot, I remembered the entire day: the way the colors shone in the aspens; the maniacal fever the dogs possessed in performing their greatest desire; a staunch point by a veteran setter on the other side of the hill of her hunting career; a smart shot from a treasured gun saved for days precisely like this one; and a determined retrieve by a young dog that turned into the seasoned veteran of the family. And the proud realization that I was more like my father than I'd perceived, on the road to becoming the man he wanted me to be. If I had taken the shot, I would have remembered only the shot.

We closed the brilliant October Third with a few pictures, and at home, I gladly cleaned the bird while Dad fingered a few ice cubes in an inch of scotch and rubbed a well-oiled cloth over the English gun's barrels. We talked again of the bird, and he said that the grouse rocketed ahead of him – sportingly enough indeed. "But it made the mistake of flying straightaway." A mistake not to be made in front of the Scott and Dad. "Still, I can't believe I didn't hit him harder," he declared.

"Oh well, Mags got a great fetch out of it," I replied. Curled next to me while I cleaned the bird, she thumped her tail at the mention of her name.

"And Jess made two nice points – one on the bird, and one on the cripple. We never would've found that bird without 'em," he said, smiling down at Jess, who, after taking a few sips of Dad's scotch, stretched out on his hunting vest.

"C'mon upstairs when you're finished," he muttered to me. "Mom's got some dinner waiting."

—Jake Smith

Earth Day

Earth Day dawned cold, gray, and damp this year. It was fitting to the melancholy I felt, because I knew what lay ahead. We were about to bury Carl VanderWall – Emmet County Conservation Officer and loving father of my two daughters' dear friends, Ahna and Noel. But Carl wasn't just leaving his daughters behind. He was also leaving two sons, Jaden and Noah, as well as his loving wife, Jennifer. Cancer took him from his family at age 42. My prayers for his healing of the past year were not answered in the way I wanted, and now I prayed for one last thing: sunshine.

It seemed fitting that this man, who made a career of protecting wildlife and the environment, be buried on Earth Day. I had hopes of a bright spring day to help everyone's gloom, but Friday April 22 was far from it. The weather this spring had paralleled the roller coaster ride that Carl and his family experienced in the last year as he was diagnosed with brain cancer. Prayers were answered. Doors were opened. Miracles happened. The cancer was gone without a trace.

And then it returned. I don't know why God would take such a loving father, coach, and dedicated CO from our Earth. I've given up pretending to have all the answers about faith. I know very little. Still, I believe.

It was the trucks that first struck me. The night before, we pulled into the visitation at Walloon Lake Community Church, and two black CO Silverados stood high on the grass bank before the church, flanking the parking lot entrance like silent statues, bearing testimony to the seriousness of this occasion. About eight more were neatly parked between them, down in the lot proper. Then I noticed the uniformed officers wearing the gray and green, but this time with white gloves, standing at every door to the church, and I thought to myself, *This is what it means to belong. This is what happens when you die in the arms of a brotherhood of protectors. Protectors of wild places, protectors of animals, and protectors of one another.*

The ceremony and honor bestowed on Carl and his family by the men and women wearing the gray and green at the visitation was powerful, visceral, concrete. It was just a foretaste of what would come the next day at the funeral. In the midmorning gloom, I pulled in to the church to see what I can only describe as a legion of black Silverados. Over 125 conservation officers were on hand to pay tribute. During times of grief and stress, humor helps. I turned to Brian Shaw, a childhood friend of Carl's and said, "I just feel like I should be out poaching something."

Without missing a beat, he responded, "Some people think free fishing weekend is yet to come, but today's the day."

The brotherhood of COs brought the grief to the surface that I was trying to hold down. Two of them stood at attention on either side of Carl's casket, and every ten minutes, two more marched down to replace them, silently saluting, measuring every step, every move, never leaving Carl alone. When the funeral began, the entire group of uniformed officers marched in to the mournful but powerful notes of a Scottish piper, and they filled row after row after row. Carl's partner, Duane Budreau spoke. He spoke of the integrity of Carl and his unwavering belief in right and wrong. He spoke of a man who had been arrested four times by Carl, but who still showed up last spring at Carl's benefit dinner in order to share his financial support for the very CO who arrested him. He spoke of losing a brother.

I saw many things that day that I will never forget. I saw my daughter, standing next to Ahna, comforting her with her hand on her back, moments before her father's casket was closed. I saw a young girl who tried to honor her coach by sharing that this was her first year in wrestling, and Coach VanderWall encouraged her with the words, "Every day you're improving." But her voice broke as did other young athletes who tried to speak words of love of their coach. I saw a funeral escort of black Silverados followed by Michigan state troopers, Petoskey city police, Odawa tribal police, and members of the Emmet County sheriff's department. I saw a casket cover spray painted in '80s-style green leaf template camo. I saw 125 Michigan Conservation Officers standing in rows, at attention, on the lawn of Greenwood Ceremony to honor their friend and brother, Carl VanderWall. And I cried. Not for Carl, who is healed and rejoicing in the arms of his savior, Jesus Christ, but for his children, his family, his friends, and his colleagues who now are all coping with the pain of losing someone they loved.

But I also saw the sun come out. It shone over Carl, his family, and his friends. It shone over all the officers there to honor him. And there atop the hill overlooking Little Traverse Bay, amid the gulls soaring and the crows calling and the clouds floating by, amid all the promises of spring in northern Michigan, Carl VanderWall was laid to rest on Earth Day. Soon, I will fish for browns and rainbows and brookies in the warm spring sunshine, but for now I'm content to remember a Conservation Officer and all he meant to the community who loved him.

—*Greg Frey*

The Last Retrieve

Regardless of age, every waterfowl dog has a last retrieve. If you're lucky – or unlucky, depending on your point of view – you've taken your beloved buddy out for his or her final fetch, knowing neither of you would walk this path together again.

To push an old dog past her limits during a hunt, though, in a vain attempt to squeak out one more memory, seems a bit selfish to me. While a veteran bird dog loves the game as much – if not more – than we do, there's still a crucial "know when to say when" moment only we can call; they'll go until they drop. These dogs come to us for the purpose of hunting, sure, but they quickly weave themselves into every fabric of our lives, hunting playing but a small part. There's a lot to be said for allowing an old war horse to finish out his remaining years basking in comfort, concerned only with which one of the kids' beds to sneak onto when they're at school, or refining begging skills to the rank of Jedi master.

But our decision of when to call it quits for our canine hunting buddy is tricky, almost like a pro athlete who believes his body can still do what his mind knows it can't. We've all seen them – some pitcher or quarterback who thought he finally had the game figured out with the culmination of a Super Bowl ring or World Series trophy, only to hang on for three more losing seasons and retire as an afterthought. They didn't have the foresight or class to go out on top.

When injury or illness shortens our bird dog's days afield, the decision is at least easier. Standards change quickly, and comfort – not another greenhead – takes precedence. While we mourn an abbreviated hunting life, the actual choice is simple. The tough ones occur when an otherwise healthy but gray-faced companion – aging and sore, like us – still longs to answer the bell. It's heartbreaking to hear my old black Lab, Mabel, arthritic in two legs and us trying desperately to avoid another CCL tear, whine softy on the front deck when a flock of Canadas honks overhead on their way back to the roost. Hopefully, she's thinking what I'm thinking, that while it would be great to be set up on that lake, it's also okay just hearing them.

These borderline decisions may cause us to push the envelope more than we should. While poetic to have an old buddy collapse at my feet with her last, hard fought-for duck, I fear I wouldn't forgive myself when depriving her of whatever remaining time she'd have left with a family who loves her dearly just for the sake of one more fetch. To relate, I love duck hunting, but would never risk *my* life for a bird.

Being observant, therefore, allows us to fully enjoy, absorb, and document that last retrieve, knowing it could be at the sacrifice of several more. Done correctly, these final hunts will be forever remembered and cherished. And sometimes, something extra special may even happen. I've been fortunate to have that moment with my last two Labs, as well as my father's.

Libby, my nine-year-old yellow Lab, had terrible glaucoma, and it was clear when she couldn't see me to handle nor the duck to fetch that we were at the end. So, through bleary eyes, we boated to a spot where at least a few buffleheads would be hanging out. Set up offshore, one of those little fellows mercifully came in for an easy shot. The bird was close, dead and kicking a little, which helped an old dog catch the movement. She handled it like all the others. But before I had time to decide if we should pack up, a goldeneye decoyed, and again, I watched my old girl do what she loved most.

As the tears flowed and I muttered a few prayers of thanks and reminisced, I noticed a lone mallard winging our way. Normally, mallards shy from our open-water setup, but for some reason that'll remain forever unknown, he made a beeline for the boat, flying over us, fast and barely in range. Realizing the potential to ruin the perfect hunt, I nonetheless scrambled for my double, and in one motion, sent him somersaulting to the water, a shot I had no business making.

In her failing eyesight, Libby had heard him fall, and somehow made the retrieve, returning to the sound of my voice. Snapping photos, I lost it when seeing – through my camera viewfinder – a band around one leg. Her last bird was a banded mallard. With more divers working the spread, there was no way another duck could improve that moment. We just sat, gun cased, me watching and her listening, while I did a poor job of holding it together.

Fast forward to this past November, on a chilly, snowy morning. Dad had brought along Murphy, his 11-year-old black Lab; though I knew he wasn't yet willing to admit it, I felt it could be her last hunt. Thankfully, a couple of mallards came over close enough, and Dad dropped one. Gently nudging her old bones overboard, Murph labored during the swim out, and even more on the return, so much that I told Dad to enjoy what would probably be her last fetch.

After the chaos of hauling an old, wet dog into a boat, I checked the bird. Another band. Unbelievable. Again, some tears accompanied the moment as we talked about Murph's life in review, and what a way it was to join the ranks of the retired.

All retriever owners get in the game for the same reason: to watch our dogs do what they were bred for. Though slight variations occur as to the specifics – upland, waterfowl, guide, trial, etc. – the love of having them at our side is shared by all. But a hard-charging retriever has only so many days afield, and if the natural order of men and dogs runs its course, we'll outlive them. Knowing when to call that last fetch a career, and letting them enjoy a welcome retirement, is a classy move we can do for a companion who's already given us all they had.

—*Chris Smith*

The Light at Middle Ground

Fall is fading fast. Naked branches click like dry bones in the wind, and the choppy, pewter-toned lake mirrors an apocalyptic sky. Winter's wrath brooks no quarter when the wicked weather turns minutes into hours, and few know its fury better than late-season duck hunters.

For centuries, Ottawa natives knew this floodplain as *Macatawa*, but practical-minded Dutch settlers later renamed it Black Lake. Its wide, turbid waters stretch nearly seven miles between the inlet and the channel leading out to Lake Michigan. In November, Mac grows mighty rough on windy days, but its fury pales in comparison to the Big Lake, where swells often top twenty feet or more. During those chaotic pre-winter storms, ducks flee the tossing waters for Macatawa's sheltered coves.

The man had lived along Black Lake for all his 68 years. Gazing through the kitchen window that morning, he strained to see the blinking red beacon at Middle Ground, but sideways sleet obscured

his view. As he poured a second cup of coffee, flocks of butterballs and bluebills skirted the near shoreline in search of calmer waters. Days like these were best spent beside the woodstove with a whiskey in one hand and a copy of Buckingham in the other.

Unless you lived to square off with the brittle cold and driving wind.

Unless you hunted ducks.

Shoulders hardened from a lifetime of rowing and a ruddy complexion marked the man as a longtime wildfowler. Never in fifty-odd years had he missed a chance at post-Thanksgiving ducks, and today was no exception. *A short, easy hunt*. That's what whirled through his mind as he swung the sack of decoys into the truck and drove to a nearby cottage. The neighbor who owned this summer home allowed the man to store his battered wooden rowboat on the beach for easy access. Like so many others around the lake, this cottage was dark and vacant through the off-season. On its windswept shore, the overturned dory blended in with a virtual armada of boats that wouldn't see water again until Memorial Day weekend.

The man's waxed-cotton jacket with its heavy wool collar felt like cardboard, but the stiff fabric deflected the sharp wind and icy snow. Pawing through a side pocket, his fingers found a dozen 12-gauge magnum shells. Late-season divers wore a thick layer of fat and feathers, and heavy No. 2s were just the medicine to penetrate their armor. Given the strong wind, the ducks would fly no matter what; decoys were more affectation than a necessity but part of this seasonal ritual, nonetheless. Just a handful of shotshells and a dozen decoys, that was all; these late-season, foul-weather hunts were a minimalist's game indeed. With a bit of luck though, he'd have his share by sundown.

Before shoving off, he grabbed a life vest and headlamp. *Little things are important in late-season hunting*, his father had always chided. Dad was long gone now, but his wisdom lived on. At this unforgiving time of year, even minor mistakes had a way of turning troublesome, even treacherous. But the man enjoyed these threadbare outings best of all. Even after all these years, the raw, unforgiving weather always left him wide-eyed and slack jawed. Nothing made him feel more like a real duck hunter than being out there among the bobbing blocks and ivory-rimmed rollers. The snow and wind and whipping water thrust him headlong into the thick of things, like some salty old bayman in a Pleisner painting.

The setting sun shone pale in the western sky as the man muscled the dory down the sandy beach. Stowing the dekes amidships, he waded out into the chop. Almost immediately, the cold crept through the thick neoprene waders. He smiled in spite of the temperature as divers traded back and forth across the mile-wide bay. The magic hour was at hand. Sleet reddened his cheeks as he rowed, and the waves lapped against the wooden hull with a rhythmic *schlop-schlop-schlop*.

The northwest wind kept nudging him off track, and he compensated with deliberate port-side strokes to hold the course.

When the Middle Ground Light loomed into view, he knew he'd arrived. The cylindrical, concrete pylon rose ten feet above the lake's surface like a miniature lighthouse. As the name implied, Middle Ground sat at the center of the lake – the channel lay three miles to the west, the inlet, three miles to the east, and a half-mile of open water separated the north and south shores on either side. Lake Mac was shallow in spots, but in 1909, the Army Corp of Engineers dredged out a shipping lane to allow the passage of barges and freighters. The blinking red beacon mounted atop the cement pillar marked a clear course and kept the ships from running aground.

Unraveling nylon cords, the man clipped each decoy to a mother-line anchored twenty-five feet beneath the surface. *Hardly enough weight for wind like this*, he mused, but the blocks stayed put and looked convincing enough in the wan light of evening. The stage was finally set. Now it was time to enjoy a pipe, but searching his shirt pocket, his fingers found only a hole where the Zippo should have been. The heavy brass lighter must had migrated down into his waders. To retrieve it, he'd have to stand up, and that meant making a pitstop at Middle Ground. Was all the rigmarole really worth the fuss? Yes it was, he decided. Like the decoys, smoking Dad's old pipe was tradition on these hunts. And besides, he'd welcome the bladder break.

Navigating alongside the pylon, a flock of bluebills tore overhead on a tailwind that threatened to snatch his hat. The wooden bow grated over jagged chunks of concrete, and he dismounted. After dragging the boat farther up, he wedged the shotgun firmly in the bow, unclipped the wading belt and suspenders, and retrieved the lighter. Working quickly, he wasted no time worming back into the protective warmth of wool and neoprene. As he dressed, he ran through a mental checklist. Details made all the difference in late-season hunting: Neglect the gun and it would jam; leave the mother-line at home and the decoys would float away; forget to wear long underwear and shiver all day; capsize in the frigid water and drown. Some of these line-items represented mere inconveniences; others amounted to a death sentence.

He'd almost run through the entire list when the unthinkable happened. In the scant seconds he had his back turned, the boat slipped silently into the water. When he first noticed, it was floating near the far edge of the riprap. Leaning out precariously, he wobbled over the yawning blackness, but the dory drifted just out of reach. In a panic, he tore off his ducking coat and swiped uselessly at the gunwale, but only succeeded in soaking the jacket and pushing his salvation farther away.

In hindsight, he should have lunged for it. He should have dived in, embraced the icy-cold water, and rowed home as fast as his hypothermic shoulders could have carried him. But he didn't, and the opportunity passed quickly as the wind pushed the vessel out and away.

A wave of disbelief and panic washed over him, like stumbling down a flight of stairs. First came an abbreviated gasp, then a flip-flopping deep in the pit of his stomach. *It's not the big things that'll get you into trouble,* his father's voice echoed inside his head; *little things can be a late-season duck hunter's undoing*. Icy shrapnel *shuuuushed* against the concrete as the rowboat faded into the dimming gray. A taste like rusty nails filled his mouth – the flavor of fear.

The man gazed out over the water at the distant, glowing cottages.

Maybe someone will find the empty boat and come looking, he thought hopefully, but quickly dismissed the notion as wishful thinking. Even if the dory didn't ship water over the side and sink, no one would find it for days, maybe even weeks. Hours were all he had, and no one knew he'd been banished out there on his own private Alcatraz.

Until then, he'd maintained his composure, but chaos consumed him now. He screamed himself hoarse in a moment of primal panic. Volume was irrelevant in wind that carried his cries away like a predatory bird. *Useless*, he seethed between clenched teeth. *USELESS!* In lulls when the gales died, he heard the lake pulsing and breathing like a faraway freighter. Then he prayed, pleading to God with all his might. He'd endured much colder conditions in the past, but there were other factors at play here. Nothing cooled a man's core temperature like the destroying angels of wind and wetness.

Hours passed. The man cowered low on the leeward side of the column, resting his trembling torso against cold concrete. Retreating deeper into his rag-wool sweater, he shivered violently. The damp old ducking jacket lay useless beside him. He idly checked the pockets but only found shotshells; the gun was in the boat, and the boat was long gone. For a moment, he considered dissecting the shells and using the Zippo to torch the gunpowder as some sort of feeble distress signal. Then again, what could they provide, a second or two of light and heat? Surely no one on shore would notice. Countless reflections dotted the lake's chaotic surface, and a few, brief flashes would simply blend in with the lights along the shoreline.

Greenish-black waves hissed against the concrete like hungry serpents. Huddled there alone, his thoughts returned to countless sunrises in far-flung marshes; of the searing hiss of redheads bombing the blocks; of mallards and blacks coming in on cupped wings. Smiling despite his situation, he recalled mornings when cigar smoke mingled with the aroma of bacon and eggs sizzling on the little camp stove. These snippets of a sporting life brought solace to his soul. They might have been *little things* to some, but they represented a lifetime of memories to him.

Suddenly, he wasn't cold anymore, he was calm. Everything would be alright. The shivering stopped, and he felt warm and relaxed, euphoric even. A flock of bluebills scudded by, bound for calmer waters. Their wings filled the air with the sound of tearing silk. Scaup always were his favorites. They were the last things he remembered before slipping into that deep, dreamless sleep that comes for all duck hunters after a long day on the water.

—*Jon Osborn*

Panfried Trout

I know this admission may get me dragged by my fingernails to the gallows by some people, but I love panfried trout. In an age when catch-and-release fishing is mandated, if not by law then by an unspoken moral code, such an admission might make a public execution an acceptable form of punishment. Or at least social media ridicule and derision. Not much difference these days.

Let me qualify: I support catch-and-release and am an ardent practitioner of the procedure. A rewarding experience is feeling the strength surge back throughout the body of a hefty trout and seeing him swim off a wiser fellow. My brother usually calls it hook-and-long-distance-release when I tell him I "threw them all back," never believing I set a hook well enough.

Fishing is a grand sport allowing the participant a rare opportunity to let his quarry go after the chase and capture. For many fish, though, especially warm-water species, catch-and-release rarely enters into the equation. Bluegill are put in live wells and buckets in countless canoes and rowboats in lake-littered northern Michigan to become scrumptious beer-battered slabs. The same goes for pike and perch. And grilled whitefish or walleye fillets on the patio? Bliss.

But when it comes to trout, stating a love for trout panfried with butter and bacon is practically heresy. These beautiful fish are to be placed gently back into their life-giving waters to slug it out with a deceitful Royal Wulff or Adams another time. However, the law allows some to be taken each day, and there are times when the mouth waters for the tender white flesh of a stream trout. And at no other time does the salivation occur the most as when on a camping trip.

The Manistee River beckoned. This long river picks its way meticulously across the northern Michigan landscape, offering a bounty of trout to the wading or floating angler. Any tackle works, but it's a popular haven for fly fishermen, with some waters designated solely as catch-and-release stretches or flies only. Nearly every kind of water is offered – riffles and fast rapids, to slow deep pools and almost still-water eddies. Browns, rainbows, and brook trout splash from underneath overhanging tag alders to the middle of the open current. Of course, the ones to be after are the ones gulping, not splashing. And there are plenty of those, too.

Chris and I usually save up a day or two to travel to the Manistee. It's too far away to fish regularly, though it most assuredly offers more fish than our hallowed Boardman – and bigger fish, too. So we plan for a weekday when the pressure will be sparse, and we head out as dawn announces a new day. The dark truck on the ride home usually contains two tired yet fully satisfied trout bums.

When it comes to camping and panfried trout, it's basically a crime to have one without the other. Friend Greg Frey conned an able boat from a colleague for one late June day back when all three of us carried fewer pounds and more hair. A part-time guide, Greg was more than willing to take the helm down the meandering Manistee; Chris and I, two of the best mooches you'd hope to never meet, gladly accepted the bow and stern positions. I think Greg just didn't want to get dunked, and he sacrificed fishing time to keep his gear dry.

We pushed off into a familiar stretch of several miles to leisurely float and fish until about four in the afternoon. If beached by then, we'd head far upstream to a slower, siltier section to see if any giant *Hex* flies would play out the evening act. If we still had river to float, we'd store the rods and use the oars to shoot down the river.

The spot where we'd wait for the *Hexes* would also be our campsite for the evening. Greg swore he knew a place that didn't require a camping permit and where a small blunt point of land extended out into the river. He even said there might be some big fish right out the tent. It would be a fine day for old friends to spend some all-too-rare time together.

But the menu for the night was rather questionable. We had food, of course, and could stop to buy some; but all three of us really wanted fresh fish. And whenever Chris and I plan on fish for dinner, we end up with fillet-o-hot dog instead. We warned Greg that if we lined up the hot dogs, we'd probably fool at least a few trout into the pan. He made it abundantly clear that even if he only got to send out a few casts, he'd provide the fare for the evening.

Greg took the oars in the middle of the sixteen-foot blat-bottom boat, and Chris the bow. He would hit the holes first, and from the stern, I'd drift a fly through whatever he missed. We gazed out across the river in the early morning while loading the gear, and fish splashed and jumped at the caddis flies hovering above the surface; some boiled at unseen nymphs and emergers. A wonderful welcome to the river for what looked to be a perfect day doused in hot sunshine.

But then we started fishing. Chris missed an early brook trout of some size, and some unbelievable knots occupied my time. Greg, shirt off and wearing a long-billed ball hat, rubbed his stubbly face and smiled. Though we didn't need reminding, he made us aware that he provided the boat and the service, all we needed to do was gather a few fish for the pan. Shouldn't be too hard, he told us. We had the fun part, after all.

"It sure is a beautiful day," Greg commented for the umpteenth time. It's always a beautiful day – or an interesting day or a relaxing day or some type of day – when you fish with Greg, usually because he has time to look around and admire the surroundings instead of watching his fishing partners hook fish. He has an unbelievable knack for constantly needling his buddies – even if it's only through a casual stare, a cheeky smile, and conversation of any topic other than fishing. Some of our favorite old outdoor stories revolve around a couple of duck hunters being incorrigible. Apparently, so are trout fishermen.

My knot woes continued, but Chris started hitting fish. The hot, sunny day had driven the trout to shade by late morning. Dry flies weren't enticing them to the surface, at least not fish of legal size. So we plopped Royal Coachman Streamers into every dark spot on the river.

Standing in the stern, I spotted browns and rainbows dart out as Chris stripped the fly back to the boat. Occasionally, one tussled it, but the fish of minimum length always threw the hook.

Greg decided now was his moment to play hero and swoop in to save the day. He beached the boat hard into shore's damp bulrushes near a popular riffle where Chris and I always managed to hook decent trout – when we weren't keeping any, of course. The water felt good on our legs while we wet-waded out to the middle of the river; Greg took his time lining up his rod while Chris and I watched for rises. Not many, but some betrayed their positions. We flogged the water with every creation in our vests until positive they were creek chubs and not trout making the commotion. I moved upstream; Chris ambled down with the current.

Greg had the whole riffle to himself. The line danced around his head in controlled loops, snapping back and forth like a whip, yet elegant, the line moving to the rhythm of the stream. It laid out flat and taut, and the light tan caddis floated on stiff hackles down the river. And again. And again. And again.

By the sixth fly change, Chris and I had taken seats on the bank to watch this Wizard of the Water. "It sure is a beautiful day, isn't it, Jake?" Chris said above the current's rush. Greg shot back a threatening glance. We knew he hadn't forgotten to lather up with sunblock – his cheeks, ears, and temples flushed a cancerous shade of red – but we offered him some anyway. Finally, a bend in the rod brought back some flesh tone, and a nine-inch brown succumbed to a small fly with no name. A quick rap from a tiny mallet to humanely kill it, and he dropped the trout in a cooler.

"Well, I don't know what you guys are eating, but I got my dinner," Greg declared upon returning. The one fish had lifted his spirits, and he pushed off from shore as if he'd proven his point.

"You said you'd catch the camp's dinner tonight," Chris pointed out.

"I said no such thing. I said *I'd* be eating fish tonight. You two lowlifes are on your own." Greg smirked. "I'm putting you into fish, it's not my fault the cooler isn't full."

"Row," Chris responded, whipping the rod with greater purpose.

Greg did want us to bring some fish to the fire, though he denied our accusations that it was just so he could eat more. When Chris finally brought in a brown, he raised it over the boat, and in a quick measure, Greg determined it was a legal fish. With surprising nimbleness, he stopped rowing, grabbed the mallet, and killed the fish with a swift blow while it hung from Chris's line.

"We're keeping it," Greg muttered. He unhooked the limp fish, and into the cooler it went.

Two more fish ended up alongside the others; none from my line. I managed to catch a few small ones, but I mostly enjoyed seeing the stream from a different vantage point. Rarely do we float a river, preferring instead to wade – and, especially on hot days, to venture out in shorts or light pants. But from the stern, I relaxed, reaching down and grabbing a hatful of the Manistee and dousing my head. I propped my feet on the edge and watched the scenery float by.

Large white pines engulfed stretches in utter blackness, and more than once we had to lie down to pass under overhanging tag alders and pine limbs. Through crystal water, I spotted trout dashing for cover when we approached. They glided over the cobblestone and sand bottom with amazing agility, their tails constantly swishing to hold their positions; then in a spasm from tail to nose, they'd shoot upstream and vanish in a swirl of sandy river bottom.

Log cabins lined the shoreline in one stretch, and I thought of how lucky those people were, to be able to fall asleep to the nighthawk's peent or the whip-poor-will's call, and to wake up to the mist rising from the Manistee. I wondered if they took it for granted, if they were only concerned about how much canoe traffic coated the river, or how much work is required of a cabin along a river. I wondered if they ever took a moment to open their eyes and their minds to what surrounded them, to appreciate the simple song of the river itself.

The allotted time arrived, and we still had water to float. We packed the rods and shot down the river to the boat launch where a truck waited. In short order, we sped off to the upstream section and our home for the night.

It was as Greg promised. After only a brief walk through aspens and alders, we found ourselves on top of a hill gazing down upon a narrower Manistee. Before us, the small blunt point, grown over in short grass and surrounded on three sides by water. It simply begged for the company of camping fishermen.

We went to work setting up camp, gathering wood for the fire, and trying to find a bare, level spot for the tents. No matter how hard you try, you'll always roll to one side of the tent, and a stubborn rock will do its worst to your back. A small price for sleeping in some of the best accommodations around.

As the sun began its descent, we stripped down to shorts and leaped into a deep hole off the side of the point. The river's chill snatched our breath. It's incredible how strong the current is when you surrender yourself to it. With my arms clasped around my knees, I bobbed like a giant buoy down the river. Finding my feet, I stood against it with no trouble, the walk back upstream easy. But let your body relax, and you'll be surprised at how terrifically powerful a river can be.

I changed into clean clothes just as the sun tickled the treetops. Dusk flowed with a seamless blend of color dissolving from the bright orange brilliance of the fading sun into the purple twilight beginning to reveal a few points of light. I hiked up the hill to get closer to the sky.

The river changes in different light. In early morning, it hides its swift current in a shroud of mist; in full sun, it's a torrent, promising a fight for those who walk in it. In the deep of night, the river holds all the cards, springing new deadfalls and opening up new holes to waders unfamiliar with its landscape.

But in the last few moments of light, the river is soft. The current seems to slow in the failing light, and all around is still, as if the whole of nature pauses to watch the sun set below the trees. It's in this last breath of day that all things take a silent reverie. And only when you're out there with the river at this time do you maybe understand what it is that brings you back time and again.

The view was stunning. I imagined a cabin on top of that hill, of waking each morning to the river's fog and falling asleep to the nocturnal creatures beginning their night serenade. I wondered if I'd take the river for granted, if I would grow tired of the whip-poor-will or the rushing water or the incessant hum of the insects. Staring down upon the winding Manistee, I decided it'd be nice to find out.

The *Hexes* never showed up, so we began the meal. We let the fire burn down to red hot coals and formed a triangle of wood, an opening in the middle. Trout are easy to prepare, requiring only an incision from the throat to the vent. Sliding your thumb along the backbone empties the entrails, and with a quick wash, they're ready for the fire.

We placed two cleaned fish in the pan, put a small pad of butter and a couple bacon strips in the body cavity, and set the pan right on the wood. The chimney of heat from the triangular opening had the fish sizzling in seconds, and they emitted a sweet aroma that made our stomachs rumble above the river. Flipping a couple times and a quick flash fire in the pan to finish the cooking, and each of us savored a fresh brown trout. The white flesh slid easily off the fragile bones, and the meal was more than we could have hoped for.

The extra fish went to the angler who donated the most to the pot. Here, Greg had no choice but to concede to Chris, and my brother took his time basking in the moment. Like receiving an award, he expressed his thanks to all who made it possible. Greg warned that if Chris didn't shut up and eat the fish, he'd cram it in a spot where the sun's been rumored not to reach too often.

The trout, surprisingly rich from the bacon juice, filled us up quickly. With an endless source of energy, perhaps from the second trout, Chris headed for the stream to "just see if anything's waiting out there." Greg and I stared into the coals while the panfried trout settled in our bellies, and along with the warm fire and darkening sky, it gently sapped away the remaining strength from our muscles. We talked of other fishing trips and made plans for more, but both of us were being soothed by the siren song of the Manistee.

In the vast ocean of space, the stars sparkled as if riding on an unseen current. The taste of the trout remained on my lips, and I wondered if the catch-and-release diehards knew what they were missing. For there are few things as satisfying as lying on your back under the stars after a full day of fishing with a belly full of panfried trout.

—*Jake Smith*

It's Not About the Buck

Author's Note: Michael Lewis begins Moneyball, *his epic account of Billy Beane and the overlooked, underdog Oakland Athletics, with the quote, "I wrote this book because I fell in love with a story. The story concerned a small group of undervalued professional baseball players and executives, many of whom had been rejected as unfit for the big leagues, who had turned themselves into one of the most successful franchises in Major League Baseball." And the same is true here. I wrote this article because I, too, fell in love with a story. Don't think deer hunting happens like this because it doesn't. But it did. Just this once anyway.*

It was a gloomy, wet Thursday afternoon as Dennis Keck left work from his job as curriculum director of Gaylord Community Schools. But that was no surprise. It had been gloomy and wet all October in northern Michigan. After an unusually dry August and September, bow season commenced in a flood of precipitation. Some drizzling mist, some light rains, some torrential downpours. One after the other. The bow season was a washout. Even if you didn't mind hunting in the rain, the thought of arrowing a deer only to have its blood trail wash away before the deer could be recovered kept some of us on the couch with a good book.

Keck wasn't planning on going hunting when he left work. Things changed when he got home. Keck lives on what's left of a once-vibrant thousand-acre family farm. The beige, two-story renovated farmhouse and six acres that sit against a twenty-acre farm conservancy were the only things left when a saddened farmer sold it to Keck after his own children and grandchildren just didn't have a connection with the land. The old farmer said, "Dennis, I don't get it. They just want the money."

As Keck drove down his gravel driveway, five-year-old Nolan raced out to greet him.

"Dad, let's go hunting!" Nolan said.

Keck had only been out three times this season, all with his oldest son. They had seen one button buck. Keck looked at the sky, felt the rain, glanced at his watch. It was 4:15.

"Well geez Bud, I'd like to, but it's really late. It's raining. And it's an hour drive to the property."

"Yeah, but Dad," Nolan insisted, mustering all the persuasive logic of a cut-rate attorney, "we *should* go hunting!"

That's when Keck's wife entered the debate. She had spent the day wrangling four-year-olds at an early childhood education program. The two older boys had football practice. She would take them.

"Dennis, why *don't* you take him hunting?"

It wasn't a question. Keck's marital instincts were more finely tuned than his hunting instincts. Keck compromised. He took Nolan hunting.

Keck's gear was ready, but Nolan's was not. He scrambled around the house, grabbing camouflage clothes, snacks, boots, gloves, and last, but not least, an iPad. Keck knew what he was facing. He didn't just have to overcome the cold and the rain. He didn't just have to outwit the eyes, nose, and ears of a whitetail deer. His greatest challenge was going to be the attention span of a five-year-old. The iPad was fully charged. And muted. Keck made sure of that.

He and Nolan climbed into the black Yukon, drove through town, got on the interstate, and headed north. Between the swishing of the windshield wipers and the hum of tires on wet pavement, Keck kept thinking, *It's so late. We have so little time. We're not going to see any deer.*

But he and Nolan remained positive, talking about deer hunting, how to stay quiet, how to look for sign. Nolan finished his snack and fell asleep. Despite his pessimism with the weather, Keck was grateful for where he was headed, for what they had. The property had always meant so much to him, even if it rarely yielded a buck.

One hundred-sixty acres. A sign at the gate says Double 80, but they call it The Keck Double 80. It was purchased by Keck's grandparents, Jack and Nannette Keck, back in 1982 when Keck was two years old. His grandparents both graduated from and worked for Michigan State University in East Lansing before moving north to Indian River to work as an administrator and business manager, respectively, at the Cheboygan-Otsego-Presque Isle Educational Service District. The original eighty acres they purchased is in Hebron Swamp, a stone's throw (if you can throw one four miles) south of the Straits of Mackinac and due west of Cheboygan. Hebron Swamp and Dingman Marsh sit side-by-side in a roadless area of about four square miles. Dingman Marsh forms the headwaters of Mill Creek, a few miles north, which today is a fully restored antique sawmill powered by the creek itself and operated as a state park by the Michigan Department of Natural Resources. The Double 80 also has a fishable pond where you might catch a bluegill or a bullhead if you're lucky, and a quiet, meandering creek.

Incidentally, Keck's property is just east of Paradise Lake, which was originally called Carp Lake. The name was changed after 1960 for reasons no one quite remembers but which probably had something to do with the Chamber of Commerce. In what amounts to an interesting compromise, the town that sits on the western shoreline of Paradise Lake is still called Carp Lake. Locals are fond of saying, "There is paradise in Carp Lake, but no carp in Paradise." I'm not sure if that's true, but I digress.

Years later, another eighty went for sale. Being untillable, it went cheap, so Keck's grandpa bought that, too. Hence the Double 80. It's a mix of aspen, balsam, cedar, and birch with a small patch of higher ground on the west end where an old barn sits next to a dilapidated, retro camper. The camper provided a place for Keck, his father, and his grandfather to sleep during the early years of deer camp. Even by back-to-nature standards in which a mice-infested, leaky-roof, gas-lit cabin can pass as a hunting camp, the camper has been condemned. No telling what sleeps in it now. Dennis and his boys commute to the property.

Having a degree in media, Keck's grandpa built a huge radio tower behind the Educational Service District, which was used to broadcast media to the surrounding schools before the Internet. That was his shining moment. But more than that, Grandpa Keck liked to save things. The pole barn on the property is where he saved them.

"If you go in there, it's like a time capsule," Keck says. "My grandpa could never throw anything away, so when technology would improve at the ESD and they were getting rid of all of this stuff, my grandpa would say, 'Don't throw it away. I'll take it.' Our barn is full of old media stuff like VCRs and computers, just stacked up high."

If you look carefully and dig through the educational fossils in Jack Keck's pole barn, you can probably find what most people would erroneously call a mimeograph machine (which used a stencil to reproduce copies) but which teachers know is actually called a spirit duplicator because it used alcohol to transfer images from a blue master sheet to the hand-cranked copies. The fumes were terrible, or wonderful, depending on your point of view.

"It got so full. It's funny. If you go out there, there's multiple lean-tos off the pole barn. My dad did all the work, so when Grandpa would say we'd need more room, he'd just add another lean-to. The last one is about two feet high."

Keck's father, Bob Keck, was a builder by trade, so he could put up a lean-to in his sleep. Bob and his family grew up in Northport, a little town on the tip of the Leelanau Peninsula. He hunted the property, but what he really enjoyed was building deer blinds, fishing with young Dennis on the pond, and caretaking the property. Jack Keck so appreciated his son's love for the property that, as he aged, he gave Bob sixty acres and put the remaining 100 acres in a trust to be shared by Bob and his three siblings.

Nolan woke up when Dennis stopped the truck to unlock the gate. Dennis helped Nolan get dressed in his hunting clothes. He loaded his crossbow, and they began the quarter-mile walk on a small trail that meandered through the swamp. The rain hadn't let up. Nolan, for his part, was patient, quiet, and curious.

Finally, they came to a small clearing about twenty-five yards wide and fifty yards long. The clearing runs down a natural lowland ridge that separates the swamp on one side from Dingman Marsh on the other. Along the ridge stood a few aspens, their yellow leaves now turning brown and dropping, along with a smattering of young balsam fir. Dennis had set up a tent blind not far from his grandpa's old blind.

Like most structures on the property, the blind was a bit unusual. It had a doghouse built off one wall. Jack had an old hound named

Teabury, just like the gum. He never went anywhere without his hound, so naturally when he went deer hunting, Teabury went with him. Being a thin-coated hound and having to sit for hours, Teabury would have gotten cold. When he did, he could just step through the small hole in the wall and snuggle up inside his insulated doghouse where his body heat would quickly warm the small space, keeping him content, sleepy, and quiet. Keck spent many happy hours hanging out in the blind with his grandpa, watching and whispering. But because of his failing health, Keck's grandpa hasn't hunted it in ten years.

Keck and Nolan slipped past the old blind that is slowly being reclaimed by the swamp and approached their tent blind, which gave a better vantage of the clearing. Before they could enter the blind, they first had to dodge a porcupine (a relatively easy task) that was guarding the tree upon which the trail camera was attached. The indifferent porcupine ignored them as they quietly slid the SD card from the camera and tiptoed back into the blind.

Keck has a unique set of guidelines that he follows in raising his hunters, and it's very intentional.

"I never sat with my dad with a rifle," Keck says. "When I was fourteen, it was, 'See you later. You know what you're doing. Come get me if you need me.'"

It wasn't that Bob Keck didn't love his son, and it certainly wasn't that he was more concerned about his own hunting. Quite the opposite. That's just the way things were done back then, and it's not what Keck wants for his own sons. So before Cayden, Jaren, or Nolan are allowed to shoot their own deer, they must first be in the blind with Keck and watch him shoot one. And when they are ready to shoot their own deer, Keck will be there with them, watching, guiding, supporting. Only then will they be allowed to hunt alone. But they've got a good start. Jaren is unsure of hunting, but Cayden and Nolan were each three when they first sat in a deer blind with their father.

"I typically don't shoot deer the first few times they're with me. I try to teach them how to sit, how to move, when to move. I teach them to watch the deer's behavior. Deer know the woods way better than we do, so I teach them if they jerk their heads and look back, it means something is coming. We talk about those things when we're in the blind – just watching animals and their behaviors. I want to make sure they're prepared to kill an animal – the whole process – before they just do it on their own."

Keck had hunted with Nolan before. He figured if they got an hour in, they'd be lucky. He'd first let Nolan watch and listen for as long as he could because the second step would be to break out the iPad. And once his interest in the iPad was done, it was game over, for both of them. Settling into the blind, Keck glanced at his watch. It was 5:25. As daylight savings hadn't happened yet, sunset was 6:37, with the end of legal shooting hours being roughly a half hour past that. To actually head out to the blind with an hour and a half of shooting light is questionable at best. To drive an hour to do it with a five-year-old borders on insanity.

"I'm back in the blind, it's pouring down rain, and it's not a good wind. We're sitting there. Nolan is looking and looking and nothing's happening. He stands up, and he starts moving around. He's getting restless. He makes it probably fifteen minutes before I say, 'Okay it's time to get the iPad out.'"

Keck handed Nolan the iPad. He knew what games were on it. He knew it was on mute. Keck then inserted the trail camera chip into his phone and began looking at pictures of deer, coyotes, squirrels, falling leaves, and blurry ghostlike things – anything that triggered the camera's sensor in the last week. Ten minutes later, the silence was broken by the sound of a screeching chainsaw bursting from his son's iPad.

"I look over and Nolan is playing Garage Band. Somehow he'd taken the mute off, and he's just whalin' on this guitar. *Wha! Wha! Wha!*" Like one of those Bugs Bunny cartoons where the character runs in place for several seconds before actually taking off, Keck's arms began flailing as he frantically grabbed for the iPad, trying to find the mute button. That can be infuriatingly hard to do considering those devices rotate 360 degrees and the screen always stays up so who knows which side of the machine the sound button is on, especially when you're not holding it! Finally, Keck silenced it without throwing it out the window or smashing it across his knee.

"Nolan, you *can't* do *that!*" Keck hoarsely whispered to his son. "You've got to be quiet when we're deer hunting."

Nolan shrugged with the innocence of a small child who was neither defensive nor fully comprehending. "Okay, Dad."

"That's when I look up, and forty yards out front is the biggest deer I've ever seen in the woods. Just this big, beautiful, chocolate-horned eight-point."

The deer was frozen and standing broadside, his head turned at a ninety-degree angle and staring straight at the blind. As in *locked* on the blind. Hunters know the look. It means, *Something just spooked me bad, and I don't know what it is, and I'm trying to figure out what to do, and it's probably going to include bolting in the next few nanoseconds and getting as far away from here as I possibly can.*

Keck's voice gets animated. "So Nolan is sitting next to me, and I put my hand on his chest. I'm whispering, 'Don't move... don't

breathe… don't do *anything*. There's a huge buck right out front."

While trying not to move or breathe, Nolan willed his neck to grow a few inches as he stretched to peek over the blind window. Nolan was breathing hard. Keck was breathing harder. Keeping one hand on Nolan's chest, Keck tightened his grip on the crossbow with his other, hoping upon hope that the deer would turn his head and offer a shot. Anything but disappear.

"I bet that deer stared at us for three minutes. It just sat there and stared, stared, stared. It finally spooked itself, and it did the stomp. Then it whipped to the left toward the marsh, and it took one step into the marsh where its head disappeared. I couldn't see its head, but I could see its entire body from the shoulder back. I brought the crossbow up."

Keck debated the shot. He knew it was long, but he also knew his crossbow. He had practiced out to fifty yards. He took the shot.

"When you shoot a crossbow at that distance, you hear the shot.

Then there's a delay and then a whack as the bolt hits the target. So I remember it's pouring down rain, and I hear the string *thunk* and then a second *thunk*. Its butt drops down, and it takes off into the marsh. So I'm like, *Oh my gosh! Oh my gosh!*"

Keck and Nolan sat in the blind, shaking, grinning as the adrenaline coursed through their veins, then slowly began to disappear. Keck texted his wife, Marlana. "I just shot the biggest deer I've ever shot in my life."

Then he texted his boss, Brian Pearson, superintendent of Gaylord Community Schools, and said, "I just shot a monster." Pearson, for his part, is the kind of boss any hunter dreams of having. He was at a board meeting about thirty miles south of Keck. He stepped out of the meeting and called Keck.

"You need me? I'm in Indian River. I'll come up."

Keck assured him he'd be okay.

"Well, if you do, just call and I'm there." Pearson hung up and stepped back into his meeting. He was in a suit, tie, and shiny black dress shoes. He knew the weather, and he knew the swamp. He had no other clothes in his truck. And he meant exactly what he said.

Exerting what can only be described as Herculean self-control, Keck and Nolan sat in the blind for thirty minutes, not wanting to spook the wounded deer and cause it to flee farther into the woods. Keck had pushed wounded deer before, and he didn't want to do that, not in this swamp. He shot the buck at 5:55, only twenty minutes after getting into the blind. It was now 6:25, and with the low ceiling and pouring rain, darkness was falling fast. Finally, he turned to Nolan and said, "Okay, let's go look at what we've got."

They quietly crept up to the spot where the buck had been standing. It had been at the edge of the clearing. Trails disappeared into the swamp on one side and the marsh on the other. There was no blood, no hair, and no arrow. Nothing. Keck knew they needed to get out of the area and get some help. He called Marlana and asked her to meet him in Indian River, the halfway point between the Double 80 and their home in Gaylord, so she could take Nolan home and put him to bed. Then he called his friend Gary Matelski.

"Gary, I wouldn't do this on a school night if it wasn't such a special deer, but I need your help."

Matelski agreed to ride up with Marlana so he could help his friend search before the blood trail, if they could find one, washed away.

Keck and Nolan started walking out of the swamp.

"Where are we going?" Nolan demanded.

"We've got to go home," Keck explained.

"No, we've got to go find *my* deer!" Nolan burst into tears of anger and frustration.

Keck did the best he could to explain the situation and to console his son, but Nolan was inconsolable. At Indian River, Keck carried Nolan to Marlana's car and gave him a hug.

"Trade you," he said to Marlana. Nolan got in the car, and Gary Matelski got out.

A half-hour later, Matelski and Keck were back at the Double 80. They sat in the truck for a few minutes staring into the rain through the headlights, as Keck collected his thoughts.

"It was an hour and a half after the deer had been shot, and it was pouring out. It keeps raining harder and harder, and I'm getting that sick feeling in my stomach," Keck described. Finally, he turned to Matelski, "I think we should get a tracking dog on standby, just in case."

Matelski agreed. Anything that would keep him from searching a swamp all night for a nonexistent blood trail seemed like a good idea to him.

Keck had seen a page for The Michigan Deer Tracking Network on Facebook in September. He pulled up the page and called the number. The head of the association answered, but he was down in Lansing some 200 miles south of Cheboygan. He texted Keck the numbers of the only two trackers in the Tip of the Mitt. The first tracker explained that she couldn't take the track because she was out of town. Keck called Shannon Smith, the only other tracker in an eight-county area. Smith's tracking service is called Black River Deer Tracking because her first dog's name was River and she now lives on the Black River. A graduate of Cheboygan High School, she moved downstate to Fowlerville for twenty years to pursue her career as a dental hygienist before moving back home to the northern Michigan she grew up in and loves.

Smith talked with Keck for a long time, asking a broad list of questions ranging from angle of the shot to the broadhead used. Like a good detective, that's what she does. She's a knowledgeable and experienced hunter herself, having bowhunted for almost forty years, ever since she was twelve. She gathers extensive information before making a hypothesis, making a decision, moving forward. That information can be very helpful in knowing whether to get on a track immediately and push a deer, or wait.

That information is also collected and shared within the group in a private online chat room for an accelerated education that cuts the individual learning curve to shreds. In the private chat room, they share pictures of the arrow, the hair, the blood, and the actual GPS track that the animal took, as well as detailed records of where the animal was hit, how far it went, whether it crossed water, how many times it lay down, whether they had to push the deer or let it sit.

"It's really nice to have the cooperation of the group," Smith said. "We've learned over the last few years how to handle a situation, so when hunters call us and we can't go on a track for whatever reason, we can at least give them advice over the phone as to how to handle their track. And we've made a lot of progress about tracks that we wouldn't take before that we would take now. Or we handle them a lot differently now than the way we would a few years ago. For example, we push deer now that have leg shots because we know if we push them we can catch them and dispatch them so they don't suffer through the season with a broken leg."

"She's very intelligent," Keck said. "She says, 'Here's what you're going to do. Go out to where you shot it and don't go farther than a ten-yard circle around where you shot it. If you don't find good blood, the arrow, or the deer, get out of there. I'll come up in the morning.'"

So that's exactly what Keck and Matelski did. Upon further inspection, they found a little clump of hair about the size of a quarter. No blood. But it did little to boost Keck's spirits.

"The clump of hair was laying where the trail ends and the swamp begins. It's deep, nasty, and turns into a marsh. It's not good, and I'm just sick to my stomach. I just feel terrible. We're not going to find this deer. It's raining..."

They called Smith and told her about the clump of hair. She asked them where they put it, and they told her they left it right where it lay. She said, "Perfect," and promised to meet Keck the next morning about 8:30. Keck and Matelski trudged back to the Yukon, and drove for a very dark, wet, dismal hour back home to Gaylord.

In the meantime, a group of friends had gathered at Keck's for an all-night vigil. To pray for the success of the recovery? No. To support Keck in his time of need? Not really. To play poker in his amazing pole barn man-cave? Well... actually, yes.

At a time when Keck might have wished to be alone with his self-doubt and inner torment, he couldn't. Pulling back into his yard, he was greeted by a small fleet of trucks parked willy-nilly about the barn. And then he remembered. A friend of his, a teacher from Wolverine, had asked if he could use Keck's pole barn for his monthly card club.

To call it a pole barn is somewhat of a misnomer. Technically, the 40' x 60' structure *is* a pole barn. On the outside. But a full two-thirds of the inside has been sectioned off and insulated. It's heated, too. With radiant in-floor heat. Keck spent the better part of a summer ripping rough-sawn maple and ash with a handheld circular saw to uniform widths in order to make horizontal interior siding. He cut four-inch-thick cookies from great pines upon which he attached iron legs to make three-foot-tall barstools. A massive board that still has the contours of the edge of the tree forms a bar on two sides of the room. Mounts and antlers from special deer, nice deer, normal-sized deer hold places of honor along one wall. The floor is coated in gray flecked epoxy paint – the kind we all wish we had in our garages but don't because the thought of hauling all the stuff out of your garage and scrubbing the floor makes you feel kind of weak and dizzy. A soft, gray rug surrounded by two wicker chairs with padded cushions flanks a small (dare I say) loveseat facing a big-screen TV. Yellow lampshades with deer and bear cast a soft glow throughout the room.

It's no wonder that the card club asked to crash in the pole barn. And there they were when Dennis arrived well after dark, emotionally drained and surrounded by a few acquaintances but mostly strangers. Some of them were hunters. Some, upon hearing his story, tried to cheer him up with well-meaning but meaningless guarantees of a dead buck that would be found in the morning. But others just smiled wanly, avoiding eye contact by staring intently at their cards, no doubt thinking, *You just took a forty-five-yard shot at a deer with a crossbow in the pouring rain with no arrow, no blood, and, heh, I hate to tell you, no hope of a recovery. What were* you *thinking?* Keck could have been annoyed. He could have fled to his home. Instead, he stayed up until one a.m. playing poker and wondering if he'd ever be able to live with himself. Then the poker players left, and Keck walked across the yard into his home where he tried to sleep but couldn't. He lay in bed and waited for daylight to come.

It might have been the longest, most difficult wait of his life, but there had been another wait. Worse. Far worse. A three-day wait. Keck was 23 at the time, fresh out of college, and starting his first teaching job in Naples, Florida. He had just walked in the door after school when the phone rang. It was Uncle Huey, the fire chief in Northport.

"He said, 'I've got to tell you something. Your mom passed away.'"

It was shocking, the kind of call all of us know can come at any moment but none of us want to think about. Keck's mother died of an aneurism. No one saw it coming.

"The bad part about that was, my grandparents, my mom's parents, used to live in Florida. They had planned a trip to come down and visit us and their old friends. They lived in Traverse City, Michigan. They left the morning my mom passed away. But at that time, they didn't have a cell phone. It took them three days to get to Florida. We couldn't get ahold of them. So Marlana and I had to wait three days after my mom died until they arrived. They got to our condo so excited, so happy. And I had to tell them. That was the worst day in my life, honestly. We all jumped on a plane the next day and flew home."

Keck's mother's grave is at The Double 80. So are his father's, and his great grandparents'. There is a family cemetery on the property, on one of the rare spots of high ground amidst the few shady maples, oaks, and white pines. It is on this special piece of land that family members rest, and each resting place is marked with a unique headstone that you won't find in a cemetery.

Puddingstone is a type of sedimentary and metamorphic rock that was formed a billion years ago in river channels. The soft gray matrix of the stone is filled with black, white, brown, but mostly red pebbles. There are different types of puddingstone with different names based on their geographic location. There are special varieties found in parts of England, Massachusetts, and the Straits of Mackinac. The Straits of Mackinac variety is officially called jasper conglomerate but is locally known as St. Joseph Island or Drummond Island puddingstone. However, it was the English who gave it the name puddingstone because it looked like their Christmas pudding made of boiled suet with cherries and currants in it. The infinite rock cycle slowly pushes them to the surface of the earth where their rounded snouts poke out of the ground like brown trout sipping emergers from the surface of a backwater eddy.

Over the years, the Keck family has made it a point to watch for these treasures whenever they show themselves in the woods. The puddingstones are dug up, and a plaque is attached to each one. One of them reads "Jennifer Keck 1955 – 2004." Dennis' mother was only 49.

By morning, the steady rain had weakened to a misty drizzle. Dennis got dressed, then he woke the boys for school. Upon further reflection, he woke the boys for deer tracking. It was the biggest deer he'd ever shot, and they had a special deer tracking dog coming in. He told Cayden he could miss school to go. Jaren, the hesitant non-hunter, said he wanted to go, too. Nolan insisted that *he* go. After all, in his mind, it was *his* buck. Keck had his doubts. In his mind, they were about to track a deer possibly two to three miles through a swamp filled with water that could easily go over the top of an adult's rubber boots.

Nolan protested, but Keck was right. Even the strongest five-year-old heart might not be able to will a set of five-year-old legs to walk through three miles of wetland swamp. The buck that Nolan inspired, that Nolan helped hunt, that would become known as Nolan's buck, would not be recovered by Nolan. Young Nolan Keck was getting his first lesson in the injustices and practical realities of life. He burst into tears and stormed back into the house to await the arrival of the school bus.

As promised, Shannon and her black Lab Tag arrived at 8:30. Tag was even more enthusiastic than Nolan. At five years old himself, Tag had been playing with deer legs since he was a puppy. And unlike the old adage you can't teach an old dog new tricks, Smith's former black Lab, a titled upland hunter named River, learned to be a deer tracker when he was 12.

"River loved to use his nose and find things. He didn't so much like to pick up birds or hunt birds. He didn't really like *anything* that was alive. It was kind of funny. He was always getting into things and finding things. He simply liked to find stuff. It was just something he did. So River ended up making a pretty good tracking dog."

Tag was even better. Smith had used a training method that began with throwing a deer leg, then hiding the leg, then adding obstacles and challenges such as aging the track, crossing water, and making turns. Slowly, she would try to add all the things he might come across when he was tracking. But ultimately, she needed Keck. Nowhere near as much as he needed her, but still, she did need him, or at least Tag did.

"In the end, you really have to have on-the-job experience because that's where the dog really learns."

Tag had learned a lot. He knew he couldn't chase live animals. Smith also rides horses, and Tag goes along for the ride. He will stay by her side even when live deer and elk are within sight of him across the massive fields and woodlands where she rides. While Smith said that all different breeds of dogs are used for deer tracking – hounds, pointing dogs, retrievers, mixes, even dachshunds – Labs really shine.

"All dogs have good noses. I don't think it matters the breed. I think if they have a good prey drive and they are biddable, they can make a tracking dog. But that's something unique to a Lab. They're just super biddable. They want to work for you where a hound may be more independent."

In the field, Smith took a photo of Keck's hunting license and texted it to the DNR. Within five minutes, they got approval to begin the track. Keck, Smith, Tag, and the boys followed the trail to the swamp until they got to the clearing. They paced off the shot. It was forty-three yards. Keck pointed out the tiny patch of hair to Smith, and she picked it up.

"This is a good sign," she said.

"What do you mean?"

"This is a dead deer."

Keck asked her how she knew that just from the hair. Smith explained the length and color told her all she needed to know. Longer white hair means low. Really short dark hair means high. Medium length hair with a little light, a little dark means you hit it where you're supposed to.

"But you don't ever really know," Smith said. "So many factors go into it. There's never a guarantee that we're going to find your deer."

However, they do find a lot of them. In 2018, The Michigan Deer

Tracking Network (roughly fifty trackers) found 500 deer. For their part, Smith and Tag found eight deer out of twenty-four searches.

Smith was unconcerned about the rain. While humans need those telltale splashes of blood to guide our eyes, Tag could see with his nose.

"The rain usually is not a problem unless it's a torrential downpour. The rain usually holds the scent. Dry and hot are the worst conditions to track in. So are really cold and frozen, another form of dry. You try to time your tracks until there is a little moisture in the air. If it's snowy, you try to wait until it warms up a touch, and the sun comes up and hits the snow. It's a bit easier for the dog."

Smith asked which way the deer ran. It might seem like an easy question to answer. It's not. Some interesting psychology takes place when hunters shoot a deer. Their mind plays tricks on them. Usually they are super excited and completely focused on this little point of brown upon which the crosshairs lie. Then there is the shot and the deer reacts – quickly. Adrenaline begins to course through the veins. It's amazing what hunters see and remember, or don't see and don't remember.

"Hunters will tell you stuff that just doesn't make sense," Smith said. "They'll swear to God the deer ran to the right when the blood trail goes to the left. It's just hilarious. So I ask a lot of questions."

Keck pointed Smith toward the swamp. She told Keck and the boys to stay put so they wouldn't contaminate the scent trail.

"The dog and Shannon go in. It's such a thick swamp that they go in five feet and I can't see them anymore. I have no idea where they're at. In less than ten minutes, she calls, 'Found it! It's right here.' I said, 'No way.' In my mind, the deer was gone. I didn't hit it good."

Even after Smith had reassured him with the hair, he doubted because of the rain, the long shot, the lack of arrow, and the lack of blood. Hunters know the feeling. The pain and guilt of wounding a deer are far greater than the enjoyment of humanely bagging one.

The buck had run about 100 yards into the swamp. It died midstride in an area of thick tag alders and brush with runways everywhere. The crossbow bolt had passed through a lung and the liver and then stopped when it hit a rib. But it was underwater. Only one side of its antlers and a rounded bit of hip protruded from the swamp. There was no blood between where the deer was shot and where it was found.

Keck knew the buck was big, but he didn't know how big. When he got to it, all he could say was, "Oh my gosh." The buck dressed out at 180 pounds. Keck never would have found it without Tag and Smith. They both deserved a reward.

Tag got his first. He was allowed to chew on the deer, and like his cousin the coyote, Tag went right for the butt. As for Smith, Keck couldn't thank her enough. He asked her what he owed her, and she said she usually just works for gas money. Keck reached into his wallet and gave her everything he was carrying, which was five times what she charged. In his eyes, it didn't seem like enough. How could you possibly put a just price on such an amazing moment?

Smith was glad that Keck called. It gave Tag a wonderful outing and helped him build his skills. It gave Smith the satisfaction of using her experience and her dog to help others. She wished more people would call.

"There are so many reasons why people call. I have guys who are colorblind. Some are older and physically not able to track well. I know I have people who are afraid of the dark. It's not because they're bad shots. Sometimes they're perfectly good shots. We go on heart shots where the deer didn't bleed a drop for whatever reason."

Smith handed Tag's thirty-foot lead rope to Cayden and Jaren. She helped Keck drag the buck while Tag dragged Cayden and Jaren. Smith wished them well and drove off. Keck turned to the boys. It was time to christen the knife.

The knife was a Buck folder. It was given to Cayden by Keck's father, Bob. Cayden was very close to Grandpa Bob, much of that relationship forged at the Double 80. Cayden loved Grandpa Bob, and he even wanted to look like him. Grandpa Bob had given Cayden a Jay's Sporting Goods – the Cabela's of northern Michigan – gift card for Christmas the year he died. Cayden had outgrown his gray Stormy Kromer, so he decided to buy another. Dennis took him into Jay's where he found a green plaid one that he liked.

"Dad told me Grandpa's looked just like it," Cayden said. "So I said, 'Then this is definitely the one.'"

It was the same Christmas that Keck's father developed a cough. It was no big deal. Just a cough. But it got worse.

"I had never seen my dad sick. He was one of those guys who just never gets sick. Come to find out, in January, they found a spot on his lungs, but he didn't tell me. The last weekend in January, he was coughing so bad that I said, 'Dad you've got to get this figured out.' He said, 'I know.'

"Then on Monday morning when I called him from work, he sounded so bad I called my aunt who lives down there and said, 'You've got to go check on him.' She did. When I got down there, they already had him in ICU. They did all these tests, and the cancer was everywhere. He made it ten days."

Keck's father died on February 3. His son's birthday was two days later.

"The day before he died, I said, 'Dad what do you want to get Cayden for his birthday?'

"He said, 'Why don't you get him a knife?'"

It was a good suggestion, a clear and prescient thought from a dying man who wanted to leave someone he loved something of value. Bob's father had given Keck a knife for his *birthday when he was younger, and Bob wanted to do the same thing for his grandson. Later that winter, Cayden and Keck picked out a special, wood-handled Buck folder from Grandpa Bob. Cayden had been waiting two years to use it for the first time. Like all things hunting, he and his father would share this first experience as he learned to field dress a deer.*

Jaren had never seen a deer gutted, and at this time, he might have been wondering why he came along for the ride. Keck, a sensitive and understanding father, was aware of this. Before he started cutting, he turned to Jaren.

"This is not fun. It's not a pleasant sight. If at any time you want to walk away, just do it."

Keck started field dressing, showing Cayden how you hold the back legs apart with your knees and cut through the skin, keeping the blade up so you don't puncture the stomach. Jaren turned white as a ghost.

He said, "Dad, I want to cry."

"You can cry. There's no rules in this," Keck said quietly.

"I don't want Cayden to make fun of me."

"Cayden won't make fun of you," Keck told him. "This is a moment. Do what you have to do."

He cried. And he walked away. Then he came back, looked again, and walked away.

For Cayden the smell was awful, but the knife was beautiful, sharp, efficient. He took his turn and joined in the process. He wasn't in school, but he was learning biology and anatomy and where food comes from. Real food. And Grandpa Bob was there with him all the way.

Keck's father had other thoughts before he died, and they, too, revolved around the camp.

"The night before he passed, he was going in and out because the cancer was in his brain. I said, 'Dad what do you want for dinner?'

"And he said, 'Gosh, I just want a hot dog.'"

At the Double 80, Bob's favorite thing was to build a campfire and roast hot dogs over it. So Keck ran out and got some hot dogs from a local Coney Island joint. He brought them back to the hospital room, and he and his father watched the Michigan vs. Michigan State basketball game while they ate their final meal together. Hot dogs. Just like at camp.

Finally, Bob said to his son, "Come here. I want to talk to you."

Keck's chair was already next to the bed. He slid it closer.

Bob said, "I got two wishes."

Keck leaned in. "What's that?"

"The first one is I don't want all my ashes at the farm [what Bob called The Double 80]. I want my ashes spread in the Straits of Mackinac. And I want you and the boys to build a cabin at the farm."

"Okay," was all Keck managed.

Then Bob said, "Those are my last two wishes. I love you."

He went to sleep and didn't wake up. At about four o'clock in the morning, Keck's father died. It was all very peaceful, but certainly not just. Bob Keck was 56.

Later that spring, Keck held a memorial hot dog roast around a new puddingstone on the Double 80. Shepler's Mackinac Ferry Service was kind enough to charter him an entire ferry. He took everyone who came out on the boat and sprinkled his father's ashes in front of his grandparents' house on Lake Huron.

The buck was hung, the boys were back in school, and Keck was back in the Board Office by noon. There were photos shared. Backs slapped. Keck's boss, Brian Pearson, couldn't have been happier for his curriculum director. The buck will be mounted. It will have a place of honor in the man-cave. Friends, family, and pole-barn crashing card players will admire it. Nolan may someday forgive his father for ditching him.

But the story's not over because it's only partly about the buck. Now that Keck's father has passed away, Dennis has taken over caretaking the property. He's working with the DNR on a golden-winged warbler habitat improvement project that will benefit deer, grouse, rabbits, mice, and other songbirds as well. They're opening up some roads and clearings. A tracked skid steer with a brush cutter broke through the ice in the swamp. A gargantuan tow truck and an excavator were required to extract it. The excavator used its bucket arm to lift up the front of the skid steer while the tow truck winched it out from the rear. Hebron Swamp does not like to give up anything it claims – big bucks and skid steers alike.

Keck is also caretaking his grandparents. And Keck's grandpa, the founder of the Double 80, possibly he who loves it the most, is not well. He has Alzheimer's. The Alzheimer's was bad, but it got much worse when he lost his son Bob. Dennis visits him often up in Cheboygan.

"So he'll come in and out and forget that my dad has passed away. He'll say something like, 'I haven't seen Bob in awhile.'

"Then it'll click, and he'll start crying.

"So yesterday we were talking, and he has these moments when he's really locked in and knows what's going on. I was talking with him and explaining how we are getting these roads cut through as part of the habitat improvement project because my dad was always the one who took care of everything out there.

"Grandpa said, 'Who's in charge of all this?'

"I said, 'I'm doing it.'

"He said, 'I know you own sixty of it, but you're in charge of all of it. I know that property is important to you and your family. I want to keep it in the family. I never want it to go. Promise me that you'll always keep this property.'"

Keck's grandpa needn't worry. Keck isn't about to sell the Double 80.

"That property up there? I could sell it. I could make whatever amount of money. But whatever it is, it's not worth it. That's my family property. Just being out there and doing stuff – that's more valuable to me. Deer hunting is just something to spend time with your family – to learn patience, appreciation, hard work, and nature."

How do you explain that to people who don't hunt? How do you share the depth of meaning behind a picture of a smiling dad and son alongside a deer? How do you explain that the buck is a symbol? It's a symbol of love that is being passed on from generation to generation. Love for the deer and love for the chickadees, jays, squirrels, mice, grouse, raccoons, opossums, porcupines, and coyotes that share the land where the deer live. Love for the swamps, marshes, thickets, fields, hardwoods, and pine groves. Love for the people who first took us to those places, and love for the people we take there now.

Deer hunting has *always* been about the love of a place and the people we share it with. Whether it's state land at the edge of a trailhead or your own private cabin in the woods, we all have our Double 80s. They are the places we go to be surrounded by family and friends, and the places we go when we need solitude. They are places of excitement and laughter and joy, and places of grief and healing. They are places where strained family relations can find common ground. *This* is the story of deer hunting, and the story I've been trying to tell all along. At the end of the day and the end of a life, it's really not about the buck. It never was.

—*Greg Frey*

Shifting Winds

Red digital numbers on the alarm clock glared 3:30 a.m. a few inches from his face. For twenty minutes, he'd lain sightless, listening to the occupants of a nearby pothole – mainly specklebellies and Canadas, a few dozen cranes, a smattering of mouthy hen mallards – and two cottonwood branches brushing the top of his pickup. He didn't mind. It was sleep worth missing, tucked between two shelterbelts and an adjacent, abandoned barn and tipped-over silo. The wind gathered as the prairie temperature dropped throughout the night. God bless the computerized weather voice on his portable radio. They'd gotten one right for a change.

Ten years ago, in his mid-twenties, he began going out there, to a farm whose owners were to become friends as close as family. A mutual acquaintance, long gone now, had introduced them on the phone, and he'd driven in on them late one October evening. Refusing their inviting offer to stay indoors, he made camp in his pickup in the yard below the house, near the slough. It snowed that night – several inches – and ice formed hard enough to seal the tailgate shut. He kicked his way out with both feet, rolled from the truck, shivering, into a Canadian prairie dream: skim ice on the slough edges, and a horizon line split by gray above and white, wheat-covered stubble below. He stretched, with both feet on the ground against that canvas, and gawked.

There were ducks. Everywhere. He could hear them more than see them, but shooting time was getting close, and he scurried to a pothole out back, just far enough from the last barn to be safe. Within an hour, he'd shot a limit of puddlers with more luck than skill, given the sheer opportunities. It was one of those days so good that he knew it was now part of his life, and he would have to come back, to the same place, again. The next day, his new friends forced him to stay in their downstairs guest room, a shower and soft bed serving as welcome gratuities.

But once each year, he slept by the old barn and pothole. Just him and the dog, an aging but not-yet-old yellow Lab. She was unimpressed by the geese and squawking cranes – her once-sensitive ears replaced by the invisible muffs of a life spent in a duck boat – though she'd always been rather selective in her hearing. What her body had lost to age, the ingrained lessons of repeated water retrieves and upland hunts more than made up for; and the hunter adjusted to the dog as surely as the dog adjusted to the hunter. A loss of hearing was simply the price of doing business; it did not bother them.

What did bother him was that lump – cancer. All Labs become lumpy, but this was too early, according to the vet. Too much in his life was changing. He feared what losing Shiloh would do to him. What bothered him like the lump was that the things he could rely on – this place, this truck, this dog, this season, this *feeling* – were changing.

Ever since that first trip, twenty-six hours one way, he'd fallen in love with the prairie. He'd lived for a while on the American prairie – Kansas – enjoying the wonderful duck hunting that only the Central Flyway can provide, while his fiancé finished graduate school. His bachelor apartment wasn't much bigger than the bed of his pickup, though in the fall, he was rarely in it.

After moving back to their home in the north woods of Michigan, and even with its game-rich upland forests, he still missed that vast, open country. He needed to go west at least once a year, just him and the dog and a truck full of decoys, to this place, the farm where he squatted with his crude camp. The tradition carried on after his marriage, and now, even after the birth of his baby girl. The Place was the most desolate he'd ever been, yet full of life to the limitless, unblemished horizon. Ten miles past the end of anything, with no husband or daddy duties or deadlines. Just to hunt. Just a boy and his dog.

Dad often told him he was born 150 years too late, that he should have been a mountain man, a trapper with an old hound dog, a Hawken rifle, and no use for civilization. He wasn't sure about that, though at times, it sounded perfect. Short week- to ten-day adventures would have to suffice, to keep him grounded, guiding him between the two places, one where he lived and one where he *wanted* to live. It probably worked like that for many men with a similar yearning for the wild and empty places of the world.

The farm was the only "dwelling" for a half-mile on the gravel road. The prairie provinces are like that – gravel serving as highways and as well-maintained as many paved roads. The dilapidated barn where he parked and listened to the growing wind was a mile from there – the proverbial road less traveled, and then some. Residing in a small depression, the only way to know it was there was to follow the private two-track all the way to it. The only recognizable beacon, the silo, was now horizontal after a windstorm a few years back, further isolating this little island surrounded by a sea of wheat and peas. He was alone, at last.

Working tirelessly as a semi-successful artist during the off-season, his friends often chided him about his comings and goings every fall. Mom worried about all of the hunting he did alone, as had Dad before he died. How many times had he heard him annoyingly say, "Be careful, son, the wind and the waves are heavier in November." What he wouldn't give to hear him say that now.

Last January, Dad had suffered a freak head injury while on a hunt down south, dying shortly after, a sudden meaninglessness inflicted on a master woodsman who began and fostered his son's passion for the outdoors. It was the old man who gave him $500 after college with instructions to go west. "I don't want to see you back here for at least six weeks," he said, suggesting he live out of his truck – to camp, hunt, fish, and explore. He owed him everything. The void he thought he'd adjusted to since last winter unexpectedly flooded back a few weeks ago, as September neared and the first tinges of red and yellow tipped the swamp maples. They were the best of hunting buddies, he and his Dad and brother, and it would never be the same. In the dark, while a raging wind rocked his aging truck, resting geese made the low, somber hum of a secure roost that sounded eerily like a Byzantine church chant.

He cried for the first time since the funeral.

The dog-like yelps of dozens – maybe hundreds – of snow geese barking their way toward him from high altitude snapped him out of it. In his mind's eye, he could see them whiffling down to his hidden pothole sanctuary in the dark.

Climbing out of the sleeping bag just before four a.m., he understood why the dog had plastered herself against his bag all night. It was cold, and those snows were no doubt riding a huge wave of colder weather to make them move in the night. The darkness held promise. Opening the tailgate, the wind bit his cheeks, but also carried the sound of hungry, avian excitement.

Even with a solid three hours before shooting light, time was precious. There was no rush to beat the next guy for the best spot – he was the *only* one, hunting marshes and sloughs reserved solely for waterfowl, cattle, and coyotes. But years of hunting out there taught him that crowd or no crowd, for the best waterfowl experiences, he had to be there early and become part of the marsh.

The johnboat was right where he'd left it last year, leaning up against a junked car by the rear of his friend's workshop in another abandoned lot. Such places littered the prairie landscape and provided great habitat for a wide array of species, especially a covey or two of Huns, one of his favorites. Under the boat – an old, patched, fifteen-foot beater – was a spare sack of decoys to add to the fifty he'd brought with him. Light enough to throw in the back of his truck, he learned years ago that a boat was the missing ingredient for grand shooting when foot access wasn't possible.

His favorite marsh was owned by a neighbor and guarded by those damned cattle fences with gates that required the strength of a small ox to operate. But he loved working for his birds, and a tough fence now and then only made him smile.

Following two winding ruts that looked like they'd been made by settlers' wagons, he passed the familiar cattle scratching post, then turned right and angled downward, headlights off. He could see where he was going by poking his head out the window, and it never failed to make him laugh. When he opened the door, an eager Lab bounded past him, anxiously pacing and padding here and there. The dog went everywhere with him, in and out of season.

With a full boat, he began rowing west a half-mile through waist deep water, thankfully avoiding a death march through a prairie gumbo of silt mixed with water. Geese floated all around in tight groups, and as he'd row into a gang, their chatter would silence completely, then erupt into a great lifting of wings. Taking flight in a jet-engine roar, they'd circle the pothole, often low enough to make him duck, and land again. It was one of *the* reasons he enjoyed these pitch-dark adventures.

With a couple hundred yards still to go, one of the paddles hit a rock on the bottom just as he put his weight behind it and snapped perfectly in two. He chuckled without humor, swore under his breath, hopped out into the small whitecaps, and pushed the boat the rest of the way to an island of thick cattails. By the time he arrived, he was heaving, but exhilarated.

The water was shallower there, so he deployed the decoys while on his knees to keep his silhouette low. When the eighty blocks were set to his liking, he slithered back into the boat and quietly lie in the bottom with Shiloh. Within minutes, clueless snow geese paddled through his decoys. Birds that probably hadn't seen a man before were now almost within grabbing distance. The cigar tasted better than usual as he waited for legal shooting time.

Typically, the ducks were the most eager for breakfast, and dozens buzzed his decoys before leaving the marsh. He could have limited on mallards and pintails in minutes, but they'd be back, full and looking for a place to sit and rest. That's when he'd take his ducks.

Soon, geese began lifting off for the feeding fields to the southwest. Not wanting to educate all of them at once, he let most depart, though it was getting difficult to wait as snows scooted by overhead, sometimes within feet of the boat. He remembered an old trick about professional hunters in Africa holding two extra cartridges for a quick reload against charging dangerous game. He did the same for the last of the geese that would flush at the initial shots. It worked, the first double, close, on two unsuspecting snows, a white and blue phase; the second double straight up but not much farther as the last flock hastily departed overhead in a deafening panic. White geese hardly flew over his home state of Michigan, and he always marveled at them in hand. Dad had taken him and his brother to Hudson Bay years ago, before the snow goose "boom," and they'd shot from driftwood blinds over a dozen decoys. Now he shot them alone, at another edge of the world.

A muddy yellow Lab brought the fourth goose back, and the marsh that had been so full of life just seconds earlier was silenced. But he knew it wouldn't last. Ducks were more dependable than geese, which suited him fine. He was after mallards, maybe a canvasback or two. Prairie ponds and marshes raise a variety of species, and are as much a haven for adults in the fall as for young in the spring.

From a patch of blue sky banked the first group – seven mallards – seemingly too high and fast to ever decoy on the first pass. But whiffling wings cut the air, and in a few short seconds, Shiloh was bringing back a handsome greenhead, crop bulging with peas. The next few birds were fat drakes also, then a husky male canvasback that strafed his spread with little intention of landing. Each retrieve brought him bounding from the boat with camera in hand as he always did, gathering photos for his never-ending supply of source material for

future paintings. Today, though, there was an extra motive: He felt he was likely recording Shy's last hunt in this place.

As she proudly paraded slowly back to him with the canvasback held high, a lump formed in his throat – cancerous with thoughts of what lay ahead.

He missed a couple easy ones, but then a young speck coasted in and he collected it, righting the ship. Excellent table fare, those whitefronts, especially the young ones. His shooting was relaxed – he always shot well out here. With that many birds, he simply picked his shots. A dozen mallards piled in perfectly over the shooting hole, hovering in a twenty-five-knot wind, only fifteen yards away but oblivious to the hidden boat. He eyed the closest male and squeezed. The bird gained altitude with the miss, then angled down with the left barrel, hitting the water and immediately diving, coming up downwind and making for the far shore, several hundred yards distant. He managed to wave Shy off when he realized the bird would reach cover before she would get there.

After another miss in the growing gale, he dropped a greenhead and a decently colored pintail. Then, for the next ten minutes, he watched everything pour into his setup. It would have been easy to take another; but counting the missing cripple, he already had his limit. Alone on that prairie, no one would have known if another bird was taken, but he would have.

Packing up and walking the boat to the downwind side of the pothole took over an hour, but as soon as they arrived, Shy caught a scent trail in thick cattails, and it was game on. She chased that winged mallard nearly a half hour, even though he never saw it long enough for a finishing shot. Despite knowing it would surely feed a coyote or harrier that combed those marshes, he wanted that bird. Never one to suffer cripples well, for some reason, this one bothered him more than others.

Momentarily resting by him and getting her ears scratched for a hard-fought search, Shy snapped her head on a warm breeze. Racing twenty-five yards uphill in wide-open prairie short grass to a fencepost covered by a patch of high weeds, she thrust her head down and came up with a flapping drake mallard.

He stood there triumphantly, praising his dog, the dispatched mallard held high in his hand. As the wind howled, snow geese returned to rest, and a handful of cattle sauntered over to investigate. He *knew* Dad was there. Shy was bouncing around even though she should have been spent from a hard morning in the mud, and he realized it was the last October she'd hunt. His six-month-old daughter back home had a hold on him, and he wondered if he'd ever return to his favorite place on earth. So many changes.

He smoothed the feathers out on the last mallard and laid it, almost reverently, with the others as he'd often thought Native Americans did with the game they'd taken. He was grateful. Leaning against the fencepost, tears formed again as he closed his eyes. He let the wind whip his face, and he thought of that Place, that hunt, and Shy's final retrieve. With gear packed carefully for the long, muddy push to the truck, he headed off for the farm, alone but not lonely.

—*Chris Smith*

Of Coffee and Creek Chubs

As far as flies go, the flashy Parmachene Belle hardly resembles an Adams; they look different, but they fish differently, too. Most obviously, the Belle, a classic winged wet, sinks; the Adams, a subdued, century-old dry fly, floats. Both patterns are time-tested fish catchers.

A similar comparison applies to anglers. Take Jake and me, for example: He rocks a man-bun; my head is slick as a bowling ball. Jake dons eclectic baseball caps, while I prefer vintage drivers like my grandfather used to wear (I *am* twenty years older, after all). Differences aside, we both love fly fishing, fly tying, and the myriad trappings that accompany the sport; but our unlikely friendship began with coffee well before we waded small streams in search of trout.

That's a story unto itself, but first, a brief, historical departure. Coffee dates back hundreds of years. Legend says an Ethiopian herdsman named Kaldi noticed his goats perked up after eating berries from the then-unknown coffee plant. Kaldi brought the fruit to a nearby monastery where the resident monks concocted a drink, which kicked the coffee craze into motion. However, today's definition of a decent cup of java varies widely.

Except with guys like us.

As a professional barista, Jake (not to be confused with my co-author Jake on this book) understands quality coffee. As a career cop, so do I, although to a lesser degree. We may be separated by a full generation, but we've agreed on something since the beginning: Acceptable coffee *isn't* the primordial sludge coagulating in all-night service stations, and it *isn't* the tea-like abomination percolating in church basements across the Midwest. Real coffee begins with quality beans brewed by a qualified barista, in a legitimate coffeehouse.

Coffeehouses began sprouting up soon after Kaldi's discovery, attracting artists and musicians like iron filings to a magnet. These trendy hipsters wear snug t-shirts and skinny-leg jeans and aren't bashful about spouting beat-poetry and spontaneous verse. Stereotypes being what they are, I always assumed they'd be anti-establishment, "fight-the-power" types, and I doubted if they'd accept a bald cop in mirrored Oakleys. But I was raised by hippies and weaned on strong coffee, so mingling with caffeine-charged social radicals isn't too far outside my comfort zone.

Setting my reservations aside one day, I stopped by LJs for an afternoon cup. To my surprise, the staff was tolerant, even welcoming. Soon I was visiting regularly, and I eventually crossed paths with Jake. At that time, I was writing a book about fly fishing and he was reading everything he could find on the subject. I emailed him a few chapters and tied-up some flies to start him on his way. In the interim, we chatted about fishing and our obscure appreciation for the 1980s band, Tears For Fears.

Just when I started thinking we weren't so different, I learned of the tattoo.

Body art chronicles a story, and Jake's ink is no exception. Apparently, his piscatorial prowess is legendary, although not in the conventional sense. His tat commemorates a banner day on creek chubs. That's right, *creek chubs*, kin to the lowly carp, oversized minnows living in turbid water. Burdened by this knowledge, my perception of Jake quickly moved from Coffee Wizard to Suspect Angler. Without a doubt, he was the only guy I knew with a life-size rough fish branded on his leg.

How could this happen? I wondered; then I heard the woeful tale. One day Jake and his college roommate had an epic day catching chubs, and they felt moved to drastic action. In a moment of questionable clarity, they swaggered into a local tattoo parlor, plopped down some cash, and got inked-up. Not for a minute; not for a week; not even a year. *Por vida*, as they say when someone signs on with the Drug Cartel. *For life.*

Times may be changing, but Jake's tattoo proves yet again that fact is stranger than fiction. His decision to enter into the exclusive Creek Chub Society (*for life*, lest one forget) sounded sketchy at first. In time, however, the notion seemed less radical. And in time, I warmed to the notion and decided any angler willing to go to such lengths must be alright.

I'm glad to have trusted my gut. Turns out, Jake adores trout even more than coffee or creek chubs – and that's saying something. Recently he bought a limber fiberglass rod and a handful of how-to books in hopes of specializing in small water. He's putting the time in for sure; nothing holds him back from fishing. As a college student, when he gets the itch, he goes. It must be nice; my life's filled with responsibilities, including a full-time job with bills to pay, so fishing happens when it works with the schedule – *if* it works with the schedule.

Needless to say, Jake fishes a lot, and he's successful, too. He's caught more forearm-sized brown trout during daylight hours than most guys his age. Maybe that's normal in Montana, but in Michigan, it's unheard of. I, on the other hand, learned by limping along painfully before catching my first trout on a fly. These days, in the quiet lulls between hatches, I tell myself Jake has more expendable time, finer flies, and better gear. Eventually, though, I'm resigned to the fact that he simply caught on quicker and fishes more frequently than I did, even in my prime.

Recently, Jake invited me to accompany him fishing. Imagine the 1980s version of Ronald Reagan hanging out with the 1960s John Lennon and you get the picture. We took my truck, and the only hiccup occurred when Jake tried to cover gas using Venmo. I was confused because I assumed Venmo was some kind of snake-bite remedy. Sensing my bewilderment, Jake suggested he'd drive next time and we'd call things even.

All differences aside, our impromptu social experiment worked. Along the river, we yammered about trout and fishing gear and flies – all the normal stuff anglers discuss during off-hours. He's great company, or "good people," as they say. Jake and I are different, it's true; but fly fishing isn't a contest, and it's certainly not about who's right or who's wrong. Take away our ages, hairstyles, and available free time, and there's only common ground left over. Bottom line, we love fishing – even for occasional creek chubs.

We'll always love it. *Por vida.*

—*Jon Osborn*

The Island

The wind filled in our footprints with sand, erasing in seconds any evidence of our passing. But at that moment, if you would've gazed down the shoreline, you would've found the three of us standing there, staring out into a silver-streaked blackness rumbling with the sound of pounding surf. The canoe, pulled up onto the beach, rocked as the waves crashed against the hull and sprayed over the gunwales; a black Labrador retriever, merely a shadow in the incandescent glow from the full moon, raced around in circles, eager for the boat ride to the rocky atoll in Lake Michigan.

Equally anxious, Chris asked, "What do you think?" His arms spread before the waves frenzied by the howling northwest wind. His kingdom. By the tone of his voice, I knew his vote.

I shifted in my waders. Being on the bottom of the "having-a-say" totem pole, I kept silent. My inherent fear of deep water wasn't conducive to hunting the Great Lakes, but each time, I mustered enough of a façade of courage to get me to the Island. I tucked my green coat into my waders and clasped my arms tightly around the top, ready to venture into the black water glimmering in the moonlight. And in my mind, one step closer to my doom.

Our father simply stood there, stoically, and stared for a moment, searching across the horizon line for a solitary blinking light. We stood on the shore at a tip of sandy beachfront projecting into the water, a hint of the submerged sandbar stretching out to the small outcropping of rocks and vegetation. Spotting the blinking light – a buoy guiding the massive iron ore freighters along their routes in Lake Michigan – Dad pointed to the beacon, necessary to keep us on the sandbar and on track to the Island. Wandering off either side of the sandbar meant filled waders and paddling to safety. Calmly, he

strode off into the water to lead while my crazy brother and his equally deranged Lab followed. He motioned for me to grab the canoe's stern and help him haul it along the sandbar. Maggie hopped into the boat for a ferry to the Island. I gulped, thankful for something to hold onto.

The waves swelled against the canoe, pushing it to waist high and then dropping it back to our knees. The water was relatively shallow, and, Dad leading the way, we found the sandy walk easy. In about twenty minutes, a quarter-mile of water lay behind us, and the surf crashed along the shore of the Island. Instead of guiding the boat, now we pushed it.

We'd made this trek many times before. Some opening days saw us on the sandbar at around one in the morning, an ungodly awful time to set forth on a duck hunt. But no one sleeps before opening day anyway. Besides, we'd catch a furtive nap under the wind-blown vegetation on the Island, and lying on our back, looking up at the twinkling stars was like gazing into our own personal planetarium.

Dad and Maggie ambled ashore while Chris and I kept the boat in the water. The full moon revealed boulders and rocks jutting out of the water like a pod of porpoising dolphins. Dad and Mags were swallowed up by the tall vegetation growing in sporadic clumps along the three hundred yards of dry land, but they walked parallel to us and the decoy-, gear-, and gun-laden canoe. Within a few minutes, we converged on the tip of the Island, a petering out of rocks into a maze of ankle-deep waterways, disappearing into a sheer drop-off of more than a hundred feet into the tumultuous Lake Michigan.

In a sheltered cove of rocks and vegetation, Dad assembled the gear necessary for our customary Island fire, a small twig blaze to warm those hunting the tip in the wind. At the blind, we'd take turns or sit together, whatever the birds dictated. If sporadic, Dad and I usually lounged by the fire, sipping coffee and munching on peanut-butter-and-jelly sandwiches that in my opinion, always dripped too much jelly.

This morning, while Dad reclined in the sheltered cubby, Chris and I set the spread and waited with Maggie for the approaching legal time. At two minutes to the magic moment, Dad shuffled toward us, and we all sat in silence for the coming flights of dawn.

One green-winged teal landed amid the surf outside of gun range. Rising and falling with the swells, the little duck eventually made his way into the decoys. I rushed the bird. Two shots later, it banked over the island and into the purple sky. "How did I miss?" I asked the sky, flabbergasted. "I could've sworn I saw a leg drop." I shook my head; Chris and Dad snickered at the whiff.

Maggie melted into the vegetation without us seeing, and she reappeared with the same unnoticed fanfare. After a few minutes discussing how it was one of the first teal we'd ever seen at the Island, we heard a soft thump, and looked back to see the duck lying at Maggie's feet. Apparently, she thought my shot more well-placed and pursued the bird on her own. Silently, she made the retrieve and, probably disgusted at our ignoring her, simply dropped the bird in silence. Closer inspection revealed the duck to be completely centered, having merely sailed in his last spasms of life. Yet another in a litany of examples of the virtues of a good retriever.

Mostly mallards skirted the decoys beyond shotgun range. It's always mostly mallards out there, although a hardy black duck may mingle in. Our inaugural hunt on the Island years ago found me taking home two mallards and a black duck, the experience I can distinctly mark as officially hooking me into the world of waterfowling, the deep-water fear notwithstanding. Few gadwalls frequent the Island, and even a couple of wigeon – unusual for northern Michigan – have braved the pounding surf. And the big lake always brings the possibility of divers – bluebills, broadbills, goldeneyes, buffleheads, redheads… all these and more streak amid the rocks and waves.

As the sun crested the horizon, we fidgeted in the last minutes of the dawn flights. Most birds headed back to the mainland for shelter, and in following a few high ducks back to the mainland, Chris noticed a small black dot on the sand bar, approaching.

Binoculars confirmed our fear. Another hunter. Chris mumbled his disapproval. "We've never seen anyone else out here before," he said. We'd moved to northern Michigan a few years earlier and discovered spectacular duck hunting compared to the southern part of the state for one reason alone: fewer hunters. And the places where we can hunt ducks don't require a lottery to choose a blind, nor a greedy rush to the marsh to seize up the few spots allowed by the state wildlife agency. We prospect and hunt where we choose, and we had chosen this Island time and again, unaware of other hunters.

Oh, we'd found scattered shotgun shells on the shore, mostly rusted hulls, unearthed by the wind and waves from the lead-shot years. Definitely nothing new to suggest another group of hunters also used the Island. But the unfortunate proof that, indeed, other hunters might find the treacherous sandbar jaunt and pounding surf pleasing was walking right toward us.

"Aren't there enough places to hunt around here?" I said. "It's just our luck, isn't it?" Chris agreed and then shook his head in defeat as three approaching mallards flared high after spotting the stranger.

Northern Michigan isn't without its fair share of places to hunt or fish. The large inland lakes sport nice flights of bluebills and goldeneyes late in November; the smaller lakes, especially those in close proximity to Lake Michigan, shelter swarms of birds during the big blows. A multitude of marshes and beaver ponds hold mallards, black ducks, wood ducks, and a variety of other dabblers. Ruffed grouse and woodcock coverts tucked down back road mazes boast healthy populations, and it isn't hard to find an agreeable flock of turkeys come the spring hunt.

Lake Michigan offers an excellent fishery for big boats and big fish

– lake trout, king salmon, steelhead, even smallmouth bass in the shallows around the offshore islands. A number of blue-ribbon trout streams are home to many anglers during the summer, especially when the giant *Hex* flies begin their frantic, brief life around Independence Day. The Boardman and the Manistee rivers receive the biggest pressure of fly fishermen in hot pursuit of brown, brook, and rainbow trout. But some lesser-known streams and rivers and the feeder creeks off the big lake provide jaw-dropping runs of salmon and steelhead.

So with all this land and room to roam, it irked us that someone was barging in on "our spot." He had to walk right past our vehicles to get to the sandbar, and even a glancing inspection would've revealed our purpose of hunting the Island. Chris and I turned back to the decoys; Dad walked down the shore for a conversation.

He invited the stranger to the sheltered cove to sit by the fire and warm up. The man carried no decoys or gear – just an autoloader over his shoulder, held in place by a sling. Upon walking back to the fire to meet the man, Chris and I discovered he was quite old, a shock of silver hair spilling out from under his camouflage hat and a host of wrinkles creasing his face. He rubbed his calloused hands over the snapping flames and turned his palms to the heat, thankful for a small bit of coffee from the thermos. I instantly felt guilty about the prejudgment; from the looks of it, he wouldn't have trudged all the way out to this Island without good reason.

"It's nice to see some young people out here," Roger mumbled, leaning back against a boulder. He sounded like my grandfather, and I instantly liked him, this weathered old duck hunter. Chris smiled, equally ashamed, yet intrigued.

"How long has this island been here?" Chris asked, sitting down and forgetting the decoys for the moment. Maggie leaned against him but kept her eyes peeled to the sky.

"I've been walking that sandbar for the past thirty years," he began. "Used to carry my boy on my shoulders out here every morning when he was little. When he grew older, he'd haul the gear, just like you two strapping young men," he chuckled. But something passed across his face, a fleeting glimmer of grief, and he stared at the sand for a moment in silence, as if trying to commune with his old friends – the rocks and the wind and the water. Or perhaps his son.

"Haven't gotten out much in recent years, but I always find at least one day during the season when I can walk to this island, if anything just to be out here for a little while." He turned his wind-beaten face to the water and closed his eyes, recalling the memories. "Wife's pretty sick. Aren't many days left when I can leave her alone for a bit. Not many days left at all," he muttered.

A few mallards zipped by in a tailwind, and a youthful glint came back into his eyes when he spied them, his lips turning up at the corners. We invited him to sit near the decoys, and he dropped a mallard that Chris called in. Maggie delivered the bird to her owner, who presented it to Roger. The old man stood in awe of the bird, his eyes poring over the feathers and a trembly hand smoothing them down. He scratched Maggie's head in thanks, and she lowered her ears in a Labrador smile; then he returned to the fire and its warmth.

The birds started to fly, though Roger was content with his one mallard and the small fire. Dad joined us on the tip, where he quickly dispatched two single mallards in a few minutes, each bird cupping into the spread in response to Chris's expert calling.

"See, I like to keep this other barrel for my Rolaids," Dad informed us, withdrawing a smoking shell from his right barrel. "Less to clean that way." Maggie deposited the drake mallard into his hand. Before inspecting the bird, he made sure to rub the Lab's wet ears in thanks. Grasping both birds by their orange feet, he turned back to the fire. "I'm ready to go whenever you guys are. Please don't tell me you're going to make me wait out here until you put on a performance such as that which you've just witnessed. I'd like my grandchildren to see me before they go off to college." With that, he walked back to the sheltered cove and the warmth of the fire and Roger's company.

In the breakers on the tip of the Island, Chris caught a flash of white streaking past, and a drake goldeneye skirted the last tolling decoy and curved toward us, racing down the line of bluebill blocks. I ended a whispered argument of whose shot it was by reminding Chris he hadn't fired his gun yet; he calmly stood and sent a spray of water behind the bird with the first shot but caught up and tumbled him with the second. Maggie bounded forth, the waves crashing on her head and back. As she approached, the bird dove in a last attempt to escape. The seasoned black dog simply submerged after it and resurfaced holding a mouthful of duck butt. I clapped Chris on the back, and after settling back into the sparse vegetation serving as our blind, we scanned the waves again for more divers.

But a hoarse quack sounded above the surf: a lone black duck raced overhead with the wind. Once out over the lake, the bird spotted the decoys and turned into the gale, beating his wings furiously. He dropped altitude to a few feet off the deck and coasted into the mallard spread. Displaying an unaccustomed degree of competency, I stood and splashed the bird. Maggie, thrilled, didn't wait for Chris to give her the command to go. The wind whipped away his calls for her to come back and do it properly, and in seconds, she trotted back with the big, dark duck.

We took turns throughout the day regaining lost heat at the fire, conversing with Roger about the Island, sharing our lunch and coffee. The seasoned duck hunter appreciated the hospitality, even though he owned more rights to the Island than we. It was an old friend of his, but he saw it in new company, with new custodians, and it pleased him. "I think this island is in good hands," he muttered to Chris and me, perhaps seeing something in us he wished he would've found in his own son. Ridiculous to speculate, I know; nonetheless, we had Roger's blessing to keep the Island tradition alive.

We told Roger to wait a few minutes while we picked up the decoys so he could walk back with us to the mainland, using the boat for a bit of support. He and Dad talked some more while Chris and I climbed into the boat to retrieve the diver decoys in the deeper water.

My phobia flared. The bright sun pierced Lake Michigan's crystal-clear water all the way down to the rocky bottom, thirty feet below. Chris ballyhooed in the stern, paddling against the wind, the canoe cresting the waves and slamming back down.

"We won't get a second chance at these, Jake!" he yelled from the back. Unable to breathe, I leaned over and dunked my entire arm underneath each decoy to be sure I hooked the line. Chris *yee-hawed* through another giant swell, which sent my white knuckles clinging to the sides of the boat.

Staring into that abyss beneath the boat, it occurred to me – in a purely rational way – that a freshwater great white shark was ready to slam into the boat and drag me under. I know: I'd be an excellent case study for a whole team of university psychologists. My arm numb from the cold water and chest constricted in panic, I stumbled out of the decoy-burdened canoe onto the rocky shoreline and fell to my knees. Chris pulled the boat up on the sand, smiling insanely with the adrenaline rush.

"We almost tipped a couple times back there," he laughed, slapping me on the back while I tried to regain my breath. I desperately love waterfowling, and I will continue to hunt that island until the big lake reclaims it. But it is a brutal love.

Gathered around the trucks, the boat and gear stowed and Maggie already asleep on the benchseat of Chris' pickup, we shook hands with Roger, silently accepting the torch he passed to us, the new keepers of the Island. By the Almighty's grace, we were put in the right place at the right time to appreciate our standing in the tradition we thought we started, but one that had long been underway. Roger drove away, almost like a ghost sent for our enlightenment, and I couldn't help but think of how empty it would be to let this tradition stand only with the indelible mark of one man's life. Indeed, the word tradition is meaningless unless there's another soul to continue it.

Dad waved a gloved hand in farewell, not needing to give voice to what we all knew: that it would be the last time we'd ever see him.

—Jake Smith

About the Authors

Greg Frey is an elementary school teacher, fly-fishing guide, and freelance writer. He lives in Petoskey, Michigan. When not guiding on the Jordan, Manistee, Black, and Boyne rivers, he can be found multi-tasking between teaching fourth graders and sixth graders online. It's a lot like wrangling cats without (usually) getting scratched or bitten.

Chris Smith is a wildlife artist and author from Suttons Bay, Michigan, with an incredibly understanding wife, two kids, and two Labs. He's won just enough state duck stamp competitions to justify his hunting and fishing habits as "field research" to his family, though they grew wise a long time ago. Chris believes that God put our eyes next to each other so that we'd shoot side-by-sides, brook trout are the perfect fish regardless of size, and every outing goes better when supervised by a good bird dog.

One of the sobering epiphanies of **Jon Osborn**'s life arrived when he realized that raising teenagers consumes 97.78 percent of a given day. Since then, he resolved to divide any remaining moments among fly fishing, upland hunting, foraging, and writing. Jon, his wife, two kids, and a tri-colored setter live in southwest Michigan, where trout and wild birds exist just far enough away to make every trip afield special.

Jake Smith is the editor of *The Pointing Dog Journal*, *The Retriever Journal*, and *Just Labs* magazines, as well as the author of the family, faith, and baseball novel *Wish*. He lives in Traverse City, Michigan, with his wife, three kids, and three Labradors. You'd think being the editor of three dog magazines that his dogs would be well-trained, but they're knuckleheads.

Made in the USA
Monee, IL
08 February 2023

26763442R00072